Matteo Ricci and the Catholic Mission to China, 1583–1610

A Short History with Documents

D1520760

Matteo Ricci and the Catholic Mission to China, 1583–1610

A Short History with Documents

R. Po-chia Hsia

Hackett Publishing Company, Inc.
Indianapolis/Cambridge

19 18 17 16   1 2 3 4 5 6 7

For further information, please address
    Hackett Publishing Company, Inc.
    P.O. Box 44937
    Indianapolis, Indiana 46244-0937

    www.hackettpublishing.com

Cover design by Rick Todhunter
Interior design by Laura Clark
Voyages of St. Francis Xavier map by William Nelson
Composition by Aptara, Inc.

Library of Congress Cataloging-in-Publication Data
Names: Hsia, R. Po-chia, 1955-
Title: Matteo Ricci and the Catholic mission to China, 1583–1610 : a
    short history with documents / R. Po-chia Hsia.
Description: Indianapolis : Hackett Publishing Co., Inc., 2016. | Series:
    Passages: Key Moments in History | Includes bibliographical refer-
    ences and index.
Identifiers: LCCN 2015035222 | ISBN 9781624664328 (pbk.) | ISBN
    9781624664335 (cloth)
Subjects: LCSH: Ricci, Matteo, 1552–1610. | Jesuits—China—Biography.
    | Jesuits—Missions—China—History—17th century. | Missionaries—
    China—Biography. | Missionaries—Italy—Biography.
Classification: LCC BV3427.R46 H76 2012 | DDC 266/.2092—dc23
LC record available at http://lccn.loc.gov/2015035222

CONTENTS

Contents

9. Account of Ruggieri's encounter with Buddhist
monks during his travels in the winter of 1585–86
to Zhejiang.   59

10. Excerpts from relevant passages of *Della entrata* on
the missionary work of the Jesuits in Zhaoqing, their
relationship with their mandarin patrons, and Ricci's
scientific work.   61

11. Alessandro Valignano and Alonso Sanchez:
Two Jesuit views on evangelization in
East Asia, 1581–88.   65

12. Excerpts from letters written by Ricci to General
Claudio Acquaviva, Shaozhou, November 15, 1592,
and January 15 and 17, 1593.   69

13. Excerpt from a description of Ricci by a mandarin in
Shaozhou, written ca. 1592.   71

14. The first impression of Ricci by Qu Rukui (written
in 1599 and recalling events from the 1580s).   77

15. Excerpts from a letter by Ricci to Duarte de Sande,
Nanchang, August 29, 1595.   79

16. Translations from *On Friendship*, the first Chinese
work written by Ricci in Nanchang (excerpts).   83

17. Excerpt from *Della entrata* on Ricci's debate with the
Buddhist abbot Xuelang Hong'en in Nanjing, 1599.   85

18. Letter by the Chinese dissident and scholar Li Zhi
to a friend, in which he describes his impressions of
Ricci (ca. 1599).   89

19. Poem dedicated by Li Zhi to Ricci.   91

20. The Nanjing writer Gu Qiyuan's description of
Ricci (ca. 1598–99).   93

21. Excerpt from *Della entrata* on Ricci's 1600 journey
to Beijing and his imprisonment by the eunuch
Ma Tang.   95

22. The mandarin Feng Yingjing's endorsement of Ricci's
True Meaning of the Lord of Heaven (1603).   97

23. Excerpt from Ricci's *True Meaning of the Lord of
Heaven* (1603) to illustrate the concordance between
Christian moral teachings and Confucian texts and
Ricci's attacks on Buddhism.   99

PREFACE

The Italian Jesuit Matteo Ricci, leader of the late 16th-century mission to China, is now widely regarded as one of the most famous missionaries in world history. Much of this reputation rests on his sensitive and effective use of cultural accommodation in his efforts to convert the Chinese to Christianity. Ricci understood that any dialogue between cultures could only bear fruit on the basis of equality and mutual respect; thus, the Jesuit missionaries would first need to immerse themselves in the Chinese language, literature, history, and civilization before they could attempt to convert the Chinese. (Contrast this attitude with that of Franciscan friar Diego de Landa, Ricci's contemporary and leader of the Church's Inquisition in the Spanish Yucatan, who tortured and executed his Mayan converts, Christian neophytes all, for secretly—and allegedly—practicing human sacrifice even after their baptism.)[1] To this day, Matteo Ricci remains a symbol of the best in five hundred years of Sino-western encounters, and his memory is vivid and resurgent in contemporary China.

Unless one is fluent in Italian, Portuguese, and Chinese, however, little of this fascinating history is available to the student of history. The available English language material is flawed and one-sided. Ricci's reputation was built in large measure upon his memoirs, written in Italian during the last two years of his life in China. Entitled *Della Entrata della Compagnia di Giesù et Christianità nella Cina* (On the Entry of the Society of Jesus and Christianity in China), it was both a personal story and a missionary history. After editing this work and translating it into Latin, Ricci's fellow Jesuit Nicolas Trigault published it under the title *De Christiana expeditione apud Sinas* (The Christian Expedition to China) (1615). Trigault's enormously popular edition was translated into numerous European languages during the 17th century and sparked widespread

---

1. Over 4,500 Indians were tortured during three months of the Inquisition, while 158 died during the interrogation, 13 people were known to have committed suicide, 18 disappeared, and more were left crippled. See Inga Clendinnen, *Ambivalent Conquest: Maya and Spaniard in Yucatan, 1517–1570* (Cambridge: Cambridge University Press, 1989), p. 76.

interest in China and the Jesuits. Trigault's Latin translation itself served as the text for the 1943 English translation by Jesuit scholar Louis Gallagher. Though Gallagher's work remained the standard English version for many years, it lacked any sort of scholarly apparatus and is now considered outdated. Since then, Ricci's original Italian manuscript has been carefully edited and published (1942–49) by Pasquale D'Elia. His letters were first published by Pietro Tacchi-Venturi, S.J. in 1911. All seventeen of the texts he wrote in Chinese were published in 2001, but only two of these Chinese works have been translated into English (*True Meaning of the Lord of Heaven*, published in 1985, and *On Friendship*, published in 2009). This lack of good English translations of Ricci's own works is not the only obstacle to understanding Ricci, his mission, and his times; other than Ricci's own writings, almost no sources are available in English from the many Chinese who were Ricci's friends, opponents, patrons, and interlocutors.

The present volume fills this lacuna and attempts to redress the imbalance. Instead of portraying Ricci as a single heroic individual playing out a drama of cultural encounter on the stage of world history, this book of sources places Ricci in the historical, political, and religious contexts of the European Counter-Reformation, Portuguese Asia, and Late Ming dynasty China. Based on a fresh translation of parts of the *Della entrata*, it also offers translations of some of Ricci's letters, letters from Michele Ruggieri (Ricci's companion and mentor, and the first Jesuit to learn Chinese), selections from Ricci's writings in Chinese, and excerpts from writings about Ricci by his Chinese contemporaries. It offers students of history a comprehensive, balanced, and original text designed to engage their own critical reading of an important and fascinating period in the history of China, in Sino-western relations, and in the history of globalization.

The first part of the book, in the form of a long introduction, explains in four parts the historical significance of Ricci's mission to China. Part 1, "Portuguese Asia," describes the Iberian voyages of discovery and narrates the Portuguese construction of a network of military and trading posts in 16th-century Asia. In Part 2, "Catholic Renewal," I analyze the relationship between Iberian maritime expansion and early modern Catholic missions. I describe the role played by overseas missions in the struggle between Catholic and Protestant Europe, the relationship between different modes of missions (from coercion to persuasion), and the manner of European colonization. The activities of Francis Xavier, the first Jesuit missionary and the precursor of Ricci, are also discussed. Part 3, "Ming China," gives a succinct description of the society, economy, culture, and politics of the Late Ming as encountered by the Jesuits. Particular attention is given to those aspects of Ming society of the greatest relevance to Ricci—Confucian learning, scholarly culture, the politics of the Ming court, the world of mandarin politics, religious life in China, and the Ming policy toward maritime trade. Part 4, "Matteo Ricci," offers a concise biography of Ricci and his predecessor, Michele Ruggieri. Here Ricci's missionary approach in China is compared with that of the Spanish mode of conquest and conversion in the Americas. In addition to presenting Ricci's activities in China, the following topics are highlighted: Ricci's introduction of western geography and cartography to China; his scientific encounter with the Chinese; his religious encounter with Buddhism and Daoism; his perception of Confucian elite culture; and the perception of Ricci by his Chinese friends and opponents.

ACKNOWLEDGMENTS

I would like to thank Rick Todhunter for inviting me to contribute this volume and for his many suggestions in shaping this into a text more accessible for students and readers. This is a better book thanks to the readers for the press. In particular, Eugenio Menegon has gone beyond the call of duty to help make my work conform to the highest scholarly standards while maintaining its accessibility to beginning students. A last word of gratitude is due to Sophie De Schaepdrijver, herself a brilliant historian and the author of a recent biography on a First World War Belgian heroine, who first suggested writing a biography of Ricci. More than a decade ago, while I was almost submerged in archival research on the Catholic mission in Ming and Qing China, piloting my ship as it were on an ocean of documents with no destination in sight, she appeared as a guide. Much like the Virgin Mary for Portuguese sailors or Mazu, the Empress of Heaven, for Fujian seamen, she pointed the way to port. Write a biography. The Quincentenary is approaching. Having arrived at the far shore, I look back with pleasure and gratitude for her companionship during this voyage. To her this book is dedicated.

CHRONOLOGY

1582   Ricci arrives in Macao; Ruggieri's first sojourn in Zhaoqing

1583   Ruggieri and Ricci establish residence in Zhaoqing

1585–86   Ruggieri and Almeida travel to Shaoxing, Zhejiang

1588   Ruggieri returns to Rome

1589   Ricci and Almeida removed from Zhaoqing to Shaozhou

1590   Qu Taisu becomes Ricci's disciple

1593–94   Ricci changes Buddhist garb for Confucian robes

1595   Ricci leaves Guangdong for Nanjing and Nanchang

1595–98   Ricci in Nanchang

1598–99   Ricci's first failed attempt to reside in Beijing

1599   Ricci settles in Nanjing

1600   Ricci's second attempt to reach Beijing

1601   Ricci establishes residence in Beijing

1605   Baptism of Xu Guangqi

1610   Baptism of Li Zhizao; death of Ricci

1611   Imperial-sponsored burial of Ricci

1615   Publication of Ricci's memoirs in Latin translation by
            Nicolas Trigault

LIST OF MAPS

LIST OF DOCUMENTS

INTRODUCTION

Portuguese Asia

Six years after Christopher Columbus discovered the Americas, the Portuguese Vasco da Gama undertook an equally momentous voyage. In 1498, after months of sailing in the Atlantic Ocean, the intrepid captain rounded the Cape of Good Hope at the southern tip of Africa and became the first European to cross the Indian Ocean and land on the western shore of India. In 1510, the Portuguese occupied the city of Goa, which had been under the rule of the Sultan of Bijapur, and made it the capital of their "Estado da India"—"Indian State"—and the heart of their extensive Asian network. Portuguese Asia expanded rapidly: in 1505, the Portuguese landed in Sri Lanka; in 1510, they conquered Timor and established control over the spice trade; in 1511, they seized Malacca from its Muslim ruler, thus controlling the crucial sea passage between the Malay Peninsula and the island of Sumatra. By this time, Portuguese galleons had defeated the navies of the Sultan of Aceh in Sumatra and an Ottoman fleet in the Indian Ocean, and wrestled maritime hegemony from Muslim sailors.

In Malacca, the Portuguese met Chinese merchants from Fujian province. Following the merchants' route, the Portuguese sailed to the southern Chinese coast in 1514. The first official Portuguese visit to China by Fernão Pires de Andrade to Guangzhou (1517–18) brought along Tomé Pires, who was allowed by local Chinese officials to proceed as an emissary to the imperial capital in Beijing. This encouraging initial encounter soon turned sour. In 1519, Simão de Andrade, Fernão's brother, arrived on the Guangdong coast with another small flotilla. Attacking towns and kidnapping children, he quickly turned the Chinese against all Portuguese. Meanwhile, Tomé Pires traveled to Beijing in 1520. While Pires was awaiting an imperial audience, a petition from the Sultan of Malacca, addressed to the Ming emperor as his suzerain lord, accused the Portuguese of seizing his realm; reports also reached Beijing of Portuguese piracy on the southern Chinese coast. The unfortunate Pires was sent

1

back to Guangzhou to be imprisoned until Malacca was restored, and he died there in 1524.

Over the next three decades, the Portuguese traded and raided along the Chinese coast. They formed part of a gang of smugglers and pirates that comprised Chinese (mostly Fujianese), Japanese, and Portuguese mariners. With a main base at Shuangyu in the islands off the Zhejiang coast opposite the city of Ningbo (the chief seaport in the Sino-Japanese trade), these pirate bands operated hundreds of vessels that preyed on commercial shipping and coastal towns in China. The Portuguese traveler Fernão Mendes Pinto claimed to have visited the Shuangyu base in 1541 and described a thriving community of 1,200 Portuguese in his famous travel account, *Voyages*. It was from here that the Portuguese first sailed to Japan in 1542 and quickly established a strong trading relationship.

In 1548, a Ming fleet destroyed this pirates' nest in Shuangyu, scattering the different bands of pirates. The Portuguese moved their operations to the south, operating out of islands off the Guangdong coast and closer to their home base in Malacca. Abandoning piracy for peaceful trade, they were granted a temporary shelter in the mid-1550s in Macao at the estuary of the Pearl River and downstream from Guangzhou. Over time, the Portuguese would develop this small outpost and temporary shelter into a major commercial depot, which served a highly lucrative trade between East, Southeast, and South Asia, binding Goa, Malacca, Macao, and Nagasaki, a fishing village, established in 1550 as a Portuguese settlement in Japan.

Though Portuguese historians may harken back to the spirit of maritime adventures of old, the 15th-century voyages were really driven by one goal: profit, first in sugar plantations and the slave trade (extending these Mediterranean institutions into the North Atlantic), and then in pursuit of spices, the natural crops of the islands of Southeast Asia that flavored the dishes of Europeans and filled the coffers of their middlemen. It was in order to cut out the Muslim traders of the Ottoman Empire that the Portuguese ventured far beyond their nautical charts into the Indian Ocean. Within a generation, the Portuguese dominated the spice trade in Southeast Asia; furthermore, they had extended their trade network into the further seas of East Asia. Allied with Chinese and Japanese smugglers and pirates in the East China Seas after the 1510s, the Portuguese succeeded in establishing bases in Japan (Nagasaki) and in China (Macao) by midcentury. In this region, Portuguese traders dealt with other goods: they bought cocoons, raw silk, brocades, and porcelain from China and sold them to the Japanese, benefiting from a trade ban imposed by the Ming government on Japanese merchants—the result of violence committed by a trade delegation in 1523. Receiving payment in silver supplied by Japanese mines, the Portuguese fed the bullion famine in Ming China, where an inflationary and thriving economy was hampered by an inadequate supply of silver coinage.

Historians have called these overseas possessions "the Portuguese seaborne empire." For the 16th and 17th centuries, however, it may be more accurate to think of Portuguese Africa and Asia less as an empire and more as a series of nodal points along a very long maritime route originating in Lisbon in Europe and terminating in Nagasaki in Japan. This maritime route connected two trading networks, the larger one extending from the Atlantic to the Indian Ocean, linking Europe, Africa, South Asia, and Southeast Asia, with ships plying the sea-lanes between Lisbon, Mozambique, Goa, and Malacca, loaded with spices, cloth, slaves, and silver; and the smaller one connecting Southeast Asia, China, Japan, and Vietnam, moving silk, porcelain, and silver through Macao and Nagasaki, and interfacing with the Indian Ocean through voyages between Macao and Malacca.

Impossible to travel in one continuous voyage, a one-way journey from Portugal to India would take some six months, possibly including stops along the West African coast such as in Angola, and with an obligatory stop in Mozambique island before reaching Goa in India. The traveler, if still in good health, would wait for the monsoon winds to sail on to Malacca, and there would await more favorable winds to head on to Macao and eventually Japan, a journey that took a minimum of one year. The nodal points on this maritime route that sailed halfway around the globe consisted of fortified ports that provided shelter and provisions for the sailors and soldiers on board the sailing ships. Luanda, Mozambique, Hormuz, Goa, Calicut, Malacca, Macao, and Nagasaki were the most prominent points, some eventually lost by the Portuguese. The smaller fortifications were little more than garrison towns. But the larger ones such as Goa, Malacca, and Macao, included large indigenous populations that developed a transnational character that distinguished them from the hinterland. The Portuguese men (almost no Portuguese women ventured overseas to Africa and Asia in these centuries), brought with them servants, slaves, and associates—Congolese, Angolans, Mozambicans, Goans, Tamils, Bengalis, Sri Lankans, and other South Asians,

Malays, Javanese, Sumatrans, Moluccans, Timorese, Vietnamese, Chinese, and Japanese—in their ships. On land, they married local women and fathered mixed-blood children; they baptized these children in the Church and reared them as Lusophone Portuguese. In the larger towns, the local Portuguese population was largely creole or mestiço (whites born outside of Europe, or people of mixed Eurasian or Euro-American parentage), most of whom had never visited the mother country. Nevertheless, Portuguese institutions were re-created everywhere: in the municipal councils that balanced local interest against the royal authority represented by the viceroys and governors; in the churches and convents that preserved Catholic Portuguese identity; and in the Misericordia, the charity that allowed for the proper upbringing and honorable marriages of the girls of these mixed unions.

The temporary Portuguese shelter on the small peninsula at the mouth of the Pearl River was named Amacao, after *A ma ge*, the Cantonese name for the major shrine there. *A ma ge* was dedicated to Tianfei (also known as Mazu, born Lin Moniang in 960 in Fujian), the Concubine of Heaven, who was in life a native of Fujian and in death the chief goddess for Chinese seafarers. In time, the name Amacao was shortened to Macao, and the Portuguese dedicated it to the mother of God, the Virgin Mary, their own patroness of the perilous seas. Chaplains sailed on every *Nau*, the Portuguese name for a carrack (a three- or four-mast sailing ship), facing death with the crew on every single voyage, saying mass, administering the sacraments, comforting the sick and dying, and praying for fair and clement weather. In the retinue of Portuguese merchants one would always find priests, who ideally provided a civilizing presence among the rough-and-tumble seamen. The development of Macao, therefore, could be measured not only in the growth of its population—for which figures were sketchy in the first decades of its existence—but also by the establishment of ecclesiastical institutions. One report in 1555 puts the number of Portuguese in Macao at 300; another puts the figure at 400 plus 4 priests from the newly established Society of Jesus (see next section). These figures probably refer to white Portuguese, to which must be added a few thousand more servants and slaves of African and Asian origins. Once settled, the Portuguese also attracted traders from southern Fujian and artisans from Guangdong, who began to settle there in ever-larger numbers. Finally, there was also Mongha, a small Chinese village of perhaps a few hundred inhabitants in the interior of Macao outside of the zone granted by Ming officials to the Portuguese.

The Jesuit Melchior Carneiro (d. 1583) first arrived in Macao in 1567, the year he was consecrated for the mission territories of Japan and China. In 1569, Carneiro founded the Santa Casa da Misericordia; in 1575, he became the first bishop of Macao when the papacy made the city a diocese. The religious orders were already well represented by that time: the Dominicans arrived in Macao in 1558; the Jesuits came in 1560, and used Macao as the major base for their mission in Japan; Franciscans and Augustinians from the Philippines settled in 1579–80 and 1586–89 respectively; and female convents were established in the early 17th century. Urban development was completed when Macao gained municipal status in 1583 with the creation of a senate (*Senado*) and civic militia. This was the city that welcomed the first Jesuit missionaries who ventured into China. A profoundly Portuguese town, despite its large Chinese population, Macao retained its special character, as did all of Portuguese Asia, even after the union of the Iberian crowns in 1580, when King Philip II of Spain succeeded to the Portuguese throne made vacant by the disastrous Portuguese crusade in Morocco in 1578 that killed off King Sebastian and the cream of the nation's nobility. Fiercely defending Portuguese interests until 1640, when Portugal regained its independence from Spain, Macao maintained a close but ambivalent relationship with Manila, capital of the Philippine Islands, the largest Spanish colony in Asia. Extending their dominion around the globe, Spain and Portugal were the protectors of a Catholic Church fighting to regain its glory and influence in the Age of Religious Wars.

Catholic Renewal

In 1535, Theodor Loher (d. 1554), a Catholic monk in Cologne, lamented in his chronicle the dire conditions of the Roman Catholic Church in the Holy Roman Empire. In his native Germany, one prince after another had declared their support for Martin Luther (1483–1546), a former monk who questioned the authority of the pope and the teachings of the Catholic Church. Luther's supporters, who came to be called Protestants, fundamentally altered the religious landscape of Europe. Latin Christendom, which had stretched from Scandinavia in the north to Italy in the south, from Ireland in the West to Poland in the East, shattered. The unity of the Latin liturgy and papal obedience were no more. In the footsteps of Luther, other reformers challenged Catholicism; and close to

Cologne, in the city of Münster, a radical religious movement of Anabaptists had occupied the city with the intention of inaugurating the Second Coming of Christ and the Last Judgment; it was this event that provoked the lament of our monkish chronicler. To his consolation, the monk saw a silver lining in the gathering storm clouds: although God had forsaken the Germans, divine favor was calling to salvation those peoples in faraway lands hitherto ignorant of Christ, thanks to the maritime voyages of the Spaniards and Portuguese. The many souls lost to Protestant heresies would be replaced by a spiritual harvest richer by manyfold, as overseas Catholic missions became a major factor in the restoration of Catholic confidence and in the renewal of Roman Catholicism.

One of the major institutions in the Catholic renewal and the chief instrument for Catholic missions was a religious order established in 1534 in Paris and officially recognized by the papacy in 1540: the Society of Jesus, better known as the Jesuit order. Its founder, the Spanish nobleman Ignatius of Loyola (1491–1556), was inspired by apostolic fervor and wanted his new religious community to imitate the work of the first apostles, hence the nomenclature. Among Ignatius' earliest seven companions and followers was Francis Xavier (1506–52), the first Jesuit missionary (for a map of Xavier's travels, see p. 105).

Xavier was not only the first Jesuit missionary but also the most important missionary in Portuguese Asia. Before Xavier, the Catholic chaplains sailing on Portuguese ships had merely administered to the basic religious needs of their fellow Portuguese countrymen during the long voyages and in the various Portuguese settlements. But these clerics were not trained as missionaries and thus expended little or no effort in converting the Asian peoples that the Portuguese encountered. Xavier was different. He labored with enthusiasm for three years (1542–45) among the indigenous peoples in India before sailing to Malacca. There he met Anjiro, a Japanese samurai on the run from the law, who became the first Japanese Christian. In 1549, accompanied by Anjiro and three other Jesuits, Xavier sailed to Japan, landing in the port of Kagoshima on the island of Kyushu, under the rule of the *daimyo* (lord) of Satsuma.

The Portuguese were already known in Kyushu. In 1543, a Portuguese ship fleeing a storm sought refuge in Kagoshima; it was on board this ship that the Japanese first discovered western firearms. In a country torn by conflict between different warlords, superior European military technology exerted a powerful attraction. Thus, when they arrived in 1549, Xavier and the Portuguese were given a warm welcome. During his two-year sojourn in Kyushu, Xavier traveled to Kyoto for an audience with the emperor, who was by then merely a figurehead in the military struggles between the warlords. Hampered by his ignorance of the Japanese language and unable to secure an audience, the restless Xavier longed for yet another missionary destination. Hearing of the great riches and brilliant civilization of China, he sailed to the southern China coast. On the island of Shangchuan, which the Portuguese used for smuggling (this was before they were granted residency in Macao), Xavier awaited passage to the mainland but fell sick and died in September 1552. His missionary dream would only be fulfilled thirty years later by a new generation of Jesuits.

Xavier's career reflected the division of Europe: as a Spanish member of a new religious order founded by a fellow countryman, he traveled and evangelized in lands opened up by Portuguese traders to Asia. While the Protestant Reformation took the allegiance of many northern countries in Europe, the Iberian nations of Spain and Portugal, together with Italy, remained relatively unaffected by religious dissent against the Roman Catholic Church. While the papacy and its supporters tried to defend the old religious order in the British Isles, France, the Low Countries, Germany, Poland, and Hungary, Catholicism remained strong in the south. A Church Council at Trent (1545–63), in which the Protestants briefly participated, was intended to end the schism; it resulted instead in the permanent division of Christian Europe. Rome affirmed its teachings and traditions, offering no compromise with religious reformers of the north. In the last decades of the 16th century, a new religious fervor animated Catholicism: in Europe, this was reflected in a new combativeness and a willingness to use violence to suppress religious dissent; overseas, it resulted in a new missionary enthusiasm to bring Roman Catholic Christianity to the non-European world.

As a proselytizing religion, Christianity expanded through waves of missions in its early history: the apostolic missions in the first centuries (paid for dearly in martyrs' blood) converted the Roman Empire. After the latter's collapse, the conquering Germanic tribes accepted Christianity and eventually established a new Christian empire under the Carolingian dynasty of the Franks. Peaceful persuasion alternated with violent coercion in these centuries of Christian expansion. In the early Middle Ages, while Irish monks converted the Anglo-Saxon kings of England, and English monks in turn brought Christian civilization to the European continent, the Frankish emperor Charlemagne used fire and sword to subdue the pagan Saxons. During the following centuries, missionaries brought the Gospels to Scandinavian kings, while German Christian knights undertook crusades to force their religion on Hungarians and Slavs. With the conversion of Lithuania in 1387, the waves of Christian missions began to recede, only to swell again a century later when the Iberian Christian principalities wrestled the entire peninsula from their Muslim enemies, a process Spanish historians call the *Reconquista*—the reconquest.

Iberian maritime expansion continued the spirit of the reconquest, and Catholic overseas missions in the 16th and 17th centuries manifested the similar mixture of peaceable persuasion and violent coercion that characterized the *Reconquista's* earlier history. In their writings, Spanish conquerors of the New World expressed horror at Mesoamerican religious rituals, in particular human sacrifice, while freely documenting their own massacres of native populations. The Hispanization of the Americas was simultaneously a Christianization, since Catholicism constituted an essential identity of Spain just as Protestantism would come to characterize the English nation. The term "spiritual conquest," coined by the French historian Robert Ricard in 1933 to analyze the Franciscan mission in 16th-century Mexico, aptly describes the coercive character of conversion: no colonial conquest, no Christianization. Coercion involved not merely military conquest and political submission but also the establishment of cultural hegemony—the destruction of temples in Mexico and Yucatan, the burning of Nahua and Mayan codices, and the repression of indigenous religious practices all over the Spanish Americas. In more recent scholarship, historians have pointed to the resistance of Mesoamericans and the blending of indigenous and Spanish cultural practices, effectively rendering Christianization a process of *mesticization*, or cultural mixing. Nevertheless, coercion represented a constant presence in the Christianization of the Americas, marking this missionary territory as distinct from that of Portuguese Asia.

Colonial violence was not completely absent in Portuguese Asia. In Goa and its territories, to the extent the Portuguese could project their military power, Hindu temples were destroyed and Muslims barred from markets and cities. Though native converts were privileged over other indigenous peoples in the colonial regime, there were limits to their advancement in the Church. Native-born converts were rarely accepted into the priesthood, and the Society of Jesus—the most transnational of all Catholic religious orders—never admitted Indians into its ranks as full-fledged priests during the history of the old society (1540–1773).

The color barrier reflected the colonial race regime, and it was upheld despite occasional protests, including an eloquent letter by Matteo Ricci.

Outside of Goa and its hinterlands, Portuguese power remained limited. In addition to battling indigenous Hindu and Muslim rulers in South and Southeast Asia, the Portuguese encountered such well-organized states as Mughal India, Ming China, and Japan. They also faced ever-stronger challenges from their European rivals, as rising Dutch seaborne power in the 17th century contested Portuguese domination in Sri Lanka, Malaysia, the Indonesian islands, Macao, and Japan.

Traveling abroad primarily as traders and not as colonizers, the Portuguese differed from the Spaniards in two major aspects: they preferred diplomacy to conquest, and commercial profit, not land, was their primary goal. Catholic missions in their sphere of influence also reflected a different style. Evangelization did not have to come with soldiers; on the contrary, there was a general distaste for Castilian ways. The views of Alonso Sanchez (1517–70), a Spanish Jesuit operating out of the Philippines in the early 1580s, was anathema to his fellow Italian Jesuits working in China. Coming from the Spanish Americas and being conscious of "spiritual conquest," Sanchez thought the most effective way to open China to the Gospels was through military conquest. The idea seemed outrageous to some of his contemporaries in the Society. But given the phenomenal expansion of the Spanish Empire and the relative ease of conquest in the New World, it was not outlandish for Sanchez to dream of forced conversions after a successful invasion of China.

Ming China

Arising from the disintegration of the Eurasian Mongol Empire, the native Chinese Ming dynasty ruled over an area that comprises the heartland of contemporary China. Even with Northeast China, Mongolia, Xinjiang, and Tibet beyond its frontiers, the Ming Empire was the largest state in the world around 1400 and was surpassed only with the rise of the transcontinental Spanish Empire in the 16th century. Without doubt, it had the largest population. The official figure of 63 million people in the *Ming Shi* (History of the Ming) is a gross underestimate, reflecting the widespread phenomenon of tax evasion and nonregistration. For the year 1600, historians give an estimate of between 289 and 231 million inhabitants in the Ming Empire, a number that exceeded the combined populations of Europe, the Ottoman Empire, and Russia (the population of Europe excluding Russia has been estimated at 78 million in 1600, and that of the Ottoman Empire at 70 million in 1550).

This populous empire was divided into thirteen provinces, many as large as countries in Western Europe. Aside from the two capitals in Beijing and Nanjing, the realm was divided into 159 prefectures (*fu*), 250 sub-prefectures (*zhou*), and 1,144 counties (*xien*). At the apex of this vast realm stood the emperor, whose authority, theoretically supreme, was restrained by law, customs, ethics, and the reliance on a large bureaucracy for the governance of the realm. Indeed, the imperial civil service dominated government to an unprecedented degree. No other group in society rivaled the status of these magistrates, called *mandarins* (after the Portuguese word *mandar*, "to command") by westerners, who obtained their appointment through a meritocratic imperial civil service examination system, on which more details follow below.

Generally a sedentary group, the Ming emperors hardly left Beijing after the mid-15th century. Unlike ruling houses in Europe, the reigning Zhu family did not rely on the imperial clan to consolidate power. A system of feudatory states ruled by cadet imperial princes in the early dynasty led to a civil war shortly after the reign of the first Ming emperor, with Yongle, the Prince of Yan, a younger son of the first emperor, toppling the reign of his nephew and transferring the capital from Nanjing to Beijing. Thereafter, Ming princes received lucrative land grants in the provinces and were denied any right to participate in politics. By the end of the dynasty, the expenditure to support the tens of thousands of imperial clansmen became the single largest in the state budget. Without the help of their clan, rulers in the Late Ming often relied on palace eunuchs to circumvent the rules and culture of the imperial bureaucracy and to impose their will on the country. Entrusted with taxation, mining, the management of the salt monopoly, transportation, and even military affairs, some eunuchs rose to such high levels in the power structure that they dominated court politics. This was indeed the situation during the reign of Wanli, when Matteo Ricci sojourned in China.

Of the many different aspects of Ming society experienced by Ricci and the Jesuit missionaries, four aspects were paramount, and they will be discussed in more detail below. First, the Jesuit mission to China would have been impossible without the Portuguese, whose arrival in Ming China connected the country to the world economy during the 15th and 16th centuries. Closely associated with this economic turn is the reorientation of Ming maritime policy, which had a direct and immediate bearing on the circumstances surrounding Ricci's life and career. Secondly, rapid economic growth created a dynamic commercial society in the Late Ming. The expansion of communications facilitated commercial as well as cultural exchange. Commodities such as cotton, silk, porcelain, and rice, and such cultural objects as books, paintings, and prints circulated ever more rapidly in an expanding market. Ricci's own writings, publications, and reputation must be understood against this larger context of cultural circulation. Thirdly, Ricci's ascent in the ladder of success in Ming China is inconceivable without the consistent and strong support of officials and scholars attracted by his learning and personality. It is thus important to describe in greater detail the world in which this western missionary moved with ease and distinction. And finally, as a Christian missionary, Ricci was especially keen to understand the religious rituals and beliefs of the Chinese, albeit not without prejudice and subjectivity. In giving a brief account of Buddhism, Daoism, and the state and popular rituals, I hope to set the Jesuit mission and Ricci's own account in a more objective perspective.

When the Jesuits came knocking on the door of the Ming Empire, the Chinese had turned their backs to the sea. This was not always so. True, the founder of the Ming dynasty (1368–1644), Zhu Yuanzhang, had forbidden maritime trade in his vision of establishing a stable agrarian society. This policy of "sea ban," 海禁 *Hai Jin* in Chinese, ended in 1405. Emperor Yongle, one of Zhu Yuanzhang's sons, who seized the throne from his nephew, wanted to bolster his legitimacy by a series of diplomatic missions. The eunuch Zheng He (1371–1433), a Muslim, was appointed admiral. Between 1405 and 1433, Zheng He led seven voyages, sailing to Southeast Asia, India, the Persian Gulf, and as far west as the east coast of Africa. These grandiose maritime voyages, combining diplomacy and trade, came to an end after the seventh voyage under Emperor Xuande, the son of Yongle. In the century that followed, no official Chinese fleets embarked from the realm of the Great Ming, although merchants from southern Fujian were active in the maritime trade with Southeast Asia. Officially, the only ships that sailed to China were on "tribute-bearing missions." Ostensibly to acknowledge their suzerainty to the Great Ming, these missions from Siam, Sri Lanka, Ryukyu Islands (today Okinawa), Japan, and other countries were in fact trade missions subsidized by the needs of Ming statecraft. Over the course of the 15th and early 16th centuries, the maritime part of the tribute-bearing system dwindled in significance as other, overland trade routes assumed greater economic importance. One of these overland trade routes connected Southwest China (the provinces of Yunnan and Sichuan) to Tibet and Southeast Asia; the other was the well-established trade route between China and her central and northern neighbors. Again, in the course of the 15th century, the attention of the Ming state turned away from the seas to the steppes of Mongolia, where a revived Mongol power presented the greatest threat to Ming rule.

Despite the limited trade permitted, the tribute-bearing overland system proved grossly inadequate to handle the increasing demand for commerce from China's maritime neighbors and her own merchants. The Ming state, however, continued to restrict maritime trade, eventually declaring a sea ban in 1541 in response to violence committed by members of a Japanese "tribute-bearing mission" in Ningbo. In one stroke maritime trade was condemned as smuggling, merchants turned to piracy, and the maritime provinces—from Jiangsu in the north to Guangdong in the south—fell victim to raids by mixed bands of Sino-Japanese pirates. Repeated campaigns to suppress these pirates squandered money and lives; and a heated policy debate regarding the sea ban fueled the factional politics of the Ming mandarins. Eventually, the Ming regime adopted a mixed policy of suppression, pacification, and policy reversal. The sea ban was lifted in 1567, although only the small port of Yuegang in southern Fujian province was officially open to foreign trade. Ming policy belied the dynamics of unofficial trade, as Chinese, Japanese, and Portuguese seafarers sailed the South and East China Seas in search of profit.

The Ming was an agrarian empire, but it was a farming society with a dense network of urban centers driving commerce and industrial production. By 1500, domestic and external trade was highly developed, with the main commodities being rice, cotton, tea, raw silk, textiles, and porcelain. This last item was produced in prodigious quantities and excellent quality in the many kilns of Jingdezhen in Jiangxi province; these kilns employed tens of thousands of skilled artisans and were funded by large capital investments in advanced technologies. The other major export item was silk, or different products associated with the silk industry—raw silk, fabrics, and brocades—and eventually the Latin word for silk, *serica*, came to be synonymous with Chinese-ness itself. From the seaports of eastern China, these goods were transported to Korea, Japan, the Ryukyu Islands (Okinawa), Southeast Asia, and beyond; over the ancient inland silk routes of Central Asia, they were carried to Central Asia, India, Persia, the Middle East, and Europe.

An excellent network of inland waterways and routes carried cotton from North China to the industrial centers of the Jiangnan (southern Jiangsu and Anhui provinces, and eastern Zhejiang), which was also the most important silk production region in the world. In parts of Ming China, such as in Jiangnan and the Pearl River Delta in Guangdong, agriculture was highly commercialized and produced cotton and other commercial crops for the urban markets. Highly skilled artisans, organized into handicraft guilds, characterized these advanced economic areas.

Thus economic specialization and commerce spurred the exchange of goods. But developments in commerce and communication were also driven by the need to supply a huge garrison along the Great Wall in the north and to meet the demands for luxury in the imperial capital of Beijing. An extensive inland network of waterways connected Guangzhou in the south through two river systems to the Changjiang (Yangzi River), which in turn connected to the Grand Canal terminating just east of Beijing. Despite the slowness of water navigation, this was a secure system of communications, especially when compared to storm- and pirate-afflicted maritime voyages. Inland water-based transportation cost a fraction of what was required for overland travel using pack animals. Tens of thousands of river boats connected far corners of the Ming realm: trees felled in the slopes of the remote province of Sichuan in the southwest could flow down the Changjiang to Nanjing for shipbuilding, or be diverted onto the Grand Canal for Beijing, where palatial constructions consumed an enormous amount of wood; rice sacks traveled from Jiangnan (also on the Grand Canal) to feed the vast population of the imperial capital and the troops beyond; and foreign envoys and European missionaries, such as Ricci himself, would use these inland waterways to move about the vast distances of the Ming Empire.

By 1500, the only check to this dynamic and expanding economy was a lack of precious metals. With the modern credit system still in its infancy and extremely limited in scope—and with paper currency discredited during the inflation of the Early Ming—the supply of money depended on the production of precious metals. Thus silver was the single most important commodity in early modern China. While the country produced only a small quantity of silver, newly opened mines in Europe, Japan, and above all South America, poured an enormous amount of silver into the global economy in the late 15th and early 16th centuries. Not only did more money circulate in global trade (in terms of more and better silver coins), but silver itself became a prized commodity, with China importing large amounts from Japan via Portuguese middlemen in the 16th century and from Peru via Spanish and Chinese middlemen of the Philippines in the 17th century. The impact of a much greater monetary supply spurred the growth of the developing Chinese economy. To understand the importance of silver importation, one might usefully compare the annual production of approximately 3,750 kilograms of silver domestically in late 14th-century China, and the export of between 143,750 and 345,000 kilograms of silver annually from the Spanish Americas to the Philippines (with most of it destined eventually for China) in the late 16th and early 17th centuries.[1] The whole world was buying Chinese goods: porcelain, tea, and silk were shipped in ever-larger cargos to all corners of the world and paid for with imported silver. In the 1590s, one could buy a Chinese silk dress in Peru for 25 pesos, while a similar item of clothing of Spanish origins could cost 200 pesos.[2]

Though developing rapidly, China remained economically and geographically diverse: the highly capitalist, commercial, and industrial regions of Jiangnan or the Pearl River Delta existed alongside subsistence farming in interior provinces such as Guizhou, Ganzu, and Shaanxi. Nonetheless, the advances in communications and commerce had an overall impact on Ming culture: novels, drama, paintings, books, precious gems, furniture, and a host of other things were produced and freely bought in regional markets. The Ming government imposed very few monopolies (most notably in salt and mining), and the state usually left the market to its own movements. Compared to early modern Europe, there was almost no ideological censorship: Ming publishers produced vast print runs of works on subjects ranging from Confucian classics; romance novels; collections of poetry; model examination questions; handbooks on agronomy, hydrology, metallurgy, oneirology (the study of dreams), phonology (the study of sounds in languages), and on any number of other subjects; account books; travelogues; religious texts and prayers; to illustrated pornography. Paper was inexpensive, labor

---

1. William Atwill, "Ming China and the Emerging World Economy, c. 1470–1650," in *The Cambridge History of China, Volume 8: The Ming Dynasty, Part 2: 1368–1644*, edited by Denis C. Twitchett and Frederick W. Mote (Cambridge: Cambridge University Press, 1998), pp. 384, 392.

2. Atwill, *op. cit.*, pp. 400–01.

was cheap: a vibrant book culture in the Late Ming rapidly made literary and scholarly reputations for anyone who had the talent to offer, as Ricci would discover to his great profit.

The world of the mandarins fascinated Ricci. In one of his first letters from China, Ricci described with admiration the pomp and circumstance of their office, comparing them to ecclesiastical dignitaries in Europe. What impressed him most was their learning. These men had earned power and status by diligent studies and by passing the imperial civil service examination; they were the elites of a meritocratic system that allowed sons of farmers and artisans to rise to the top of Chinese society. In Ming China, there were approximately 5,000 provincial mandarins and another 1,000 serving in the two imperial capitals. The bureaucracies that employed the largest number of mandarins were the six central ministries (Appointments, Taxation, Works, Ritual, War, and Punishments) with some 200 mandarins, and the Censorate with some 150. Another 30 served in the prestigious Hanlin Academy, from whose ranks the Grand Secretary was customarily chosen, and about half that number served in the National University, the *Guozi Jian*. Paralleling this civil bureaucracy was the military establishment, although the military lagged far behind in prestige and influence; in the Ming, civilian officials were often entrusted with military commands, not always with ideal results. Divided into nine grades (each grade divided again into full and associate), these mandarins were at the top of a pyramid of power and prestige. They represented the uppermost strata in the social elite of Ming society, which consisted of all males who engaged in scholarship and preparation for the civil service examination.

It has been estimated that roughly 10 percent of the male population in the Late Ming had attained a high level of educational achievement, although fewer than 1 percent were certified students, and fewer than 0.01 percent had obtained the highest degree, the *jinshi*. The examination system was bound up with three degrees. At the local level, students tried to qualify for the first degree as certified student (*shengyuan* or *gongsheng* in Chinese). This status allowed the student to sit for the triennial provincial examination, held in the thirteen provincial as well as the two imperial capitals; the successful candidate obtained the degree of *juren*, which allowed him to sit for the capital examination. Also held triennially, the capital examination separated the aspirants from the successes: the degree of *jinshi*, the highest attainable academic honor, was normally a prerequisite for appointment to midlevel bureaucratic positions in the imperial civil service, such as the office of county magistrate or associate magistrate. Without the *jinshi*, a rise through the ranks to the top of the Ming bureaucracy was unthinkable. Thus a successful *jinshi* might receive his first appointment between the 7th and 5th rank, and could theoretically rise to become a Grand Secretary of the 1st rank. The fortunate few—the three to four hundred *jinshi* awarded every cycle—were given an ultimate chance for distinction: the imperial palace examination that ranked them from number one down to the second and third distinctions. These men, the *crème de la crème* of this educational system, received the most prestigious appointments in the imperial capital. For the less glorified, the *juren*, an appointment in a lower bureaucratic post was the most they could hope for in the majority of cases.

Membership in the Ming social elite was not limited to actively serving officials: retired officials enjoyed tremendous prestige in their home regions, and there were always some who preferred a private life to public service. At any one time in the Late Ming, there might have been three to five thousand *jinshi*, perhaps up to fifteen thousand *juren*, and certified students in the six figures, all enjoying different degrees of prestige in society.

Entrance to the elite came with a high cost: an individual's success, after years of studies and repeated examinations, required the focused support and investment of his entire family or kin group; it also took a heavy emotional and psychological toll on the aspirant himself. The curriculum for the civil service examination was narrowly focused on the Confucian *Four Books* (*The Great Learning*, *The Mean*, *The Analects*, and *Mencius*) along with the orthodox commentary by the Song dynasty neo-Confucian Zhu Xi—the obligatory paper topic for all examination candidates—and essays on the candidate's chosen specialization of one among the *Five Classics* (*Book of Poetry*, *Book of History*, *Book of Changes*, *Book of Rituals*, and the *Spring and Autumn Annals*). Scientific and applied subjects were excluded in an educational system that produced candidates who could write elegant essays in a prescribed form, reason philosophically, and hold forth on statecraft in accordance with the moral imperatives of Confucianism. Auxiliary skills in poetry, painting, and calligraphy were also highly prized as qualities befitting a scholar, a gentleman, and an official. The steep climb to the top of the civil service produced men of widely divergent abilities and morals: careerists scaled it successfully to accumulate wealth and power; moralists risked life and office to censor and give counsel to the emperors; those with artistic taste combined their literary pursuits with public service; while others with a religious bent sponsored pious works from their elevated positions. In the course of Ricci's quest, he would meet up with mandarins from the lowest to the most elevated rank, Chinese from divergent provincial backgrounds, and men made of different moral fiber.

Public life, as represented by studies of the Confucian classics and the duties of mandarin office, left plenty of room for the elites' private life. Many accumulated wealth; others pursued sex; some lost themselves in poetry and painting; and not a few sought spiritual fulfillment in religion. The Ming Empire was a secular state, especially when compared with the countries of Christian Europe or the Islamic Ottoman Empire. There was no official state religion, although the state did sponsor various religious rituals.

Anyone seeking to understand Ming official religion can approach the topic in one of two ways: through the ritual sites or via the classification of deities. The great sacrifices were concentrated in the two imperial capitals because their performances theoretically involved the emperor. In Beijing were the four main altars of Heaven, Earth, Sun, and Moon (which are still extant), as well as the Great Ancestral Temple (where reigning emperors made sacrifices to their ancestors), and the Great Altars of Soil and Grain. With their origins in antiquity, the sacrifices made to these major forces of nature were confirmed and elaborated upon by successive Chinese dynasties and reflected the role of the emperor as the son of heaven, whose legitimacy rested upon its mandate. While clearly reflecting the priorities of an agrarian society, the great imperial sacrifices were also devoted to ancestry, reflecting the deep filial piety in Confucian discourse, and to Confucius himself, honored as the First Teacher in temples dedicated to him in the two imperial capitals.

Mandarins in the provincial administrative centers mimicked the emperor in the capital: they made sacrifices to nature (soil and grain, wind, cloud, thunder, and rain, sacred peaks and rivers, city walls and moats) and led ceremonies honoring Confucius in the local Confucian Temple. Ritual performances, in fact, constituted one of the major responsibilities of the ruling elites in the Ming dynasty; the fact that Emperor Wanli only presided three times in the sacrifices to Heaven and Earth during his forty-seven-year reign did not put him in a high regard in concerned public opinion.

Thus Ming official religion can be usefully studied by locality; it can also be divided into categories. First, we can separate the cults into universal and local ones. All of the official cults mentioned above were universally practiced in the Ming Empire. But more local cults were devoted to meritorious officials who had done beneficial works for their jurisdiction. Some temples, such as the ones devoted to the True Martial Spirit (*Zhenwu*) or to Guan Yu, the legendary general of the Three Kingdoms (3rd century CE) and god of war, or to Tianfei, the Concubine of Heaven and patroness of sailors, were widespread if not ubiquitous. The Guan Yu and Tianfei cults highlight a conceptual challenge in understanding official Ming religion: namely, the highly fluid and changeable fortunes of a particular cult, and the difficulty of neatly compartmentalizing cults into such categories as natural or anthropomorphic, universal or local, and official or popular. Both Guan Yu and Tianfei (who was also called Mazu, born Lin Moniang in 960 in Fujian) were apotheosized; both assumed supernatural powers in Daoist and Buddhist imaginations; both spread as local cults to quasi-universal sacrifices; and both cults received official state sponsorship in the 12th and 13th centuries.

Despite attempts at state control, the Ming government neither wanted, nor was able, to define the boundaries of popular religion in a society where naturalistic and ancestral sacrifices were made by all, from the emperor down to the lowest peasant. The Great Ming Code recognized the limitations of the state: it classified religious activities into four classes, namely, those required by the state (such as sacrifices to heaven and earth), those accepted by the state (Buddhist and Daoist), those unworthy of adoption into official religion but regarded as innocuous, and those considered to constitute a threat to peace and social moral well-being, the so-called heterodox religions.

To get an idea of the extent and limitations of state control over religion in Ming China, let us turn to a brief survey of Buddhism and Daoism up to the time of Ricci's arrival. During the reign of Zhu Yuanzhang, the first Ming emperor, the state established detailed legislation for limiting the number of clerical ordinations and temples in both Buddhism and Daoism. Having served briefly as a Buddhist monk in his destitute youth, Zhu Yuanzhang rose to leadership in an army whose popular Buddhist millenarian beliefs inspired them to rebel against Mongol rule. He was thus well aware (and weary) of the subversive potential of religion and so codified state control through the creation of Buddhist and Daoist official abbots, ordination quotas, and temple amalgamation. This system decayed in the 15th century, as the state found it expedient on many occasions to raise revenues by issuing ordination certificates vastly inflated beyond the original quotas. By the 16th century, the ordination quotas ceased to have any meaning, as both Daoism and Buddhism experienced a full revival.

Three features distinguished Ming Buddhism, which experienced a spiritual and intellectual decline in the 15th century and a religious revival in the late 16th century. First, a close relationship between the Buddhist clergy and the state persisted despite the decay of the quota system; second, the distinctions between the schools came to be blurred, as the teachings and practices of the Chan (Zen in Japanese) School (which stressed meditation and sudden enlightenment) and the Pure Land School (which emphasized prayer and good works) became synthesized in the teachings of the eminent Buddhist monks; and third, the growth in lay Buddhism reflected the prominent social status of the mandarin-literati elites and their strong interest in Buddhism, and the general trend of cultural synthesis (between Buddhism, Daoism, and Confucianism) in Late Ming society.

The careers of the four prominent Buddhist masters of the Late Ming revival—Yunqi Zhuhong (1535–1615), Zibo Zhenke (1543–1603), Hanshan Deqing (1546–1623), and Ouyang Zhiyu (1599–1655)— embodied these trends. State intervention could be sudden, decisive, and unpredictable: both Zibo Zhenke and Hanshan Deqing, initially patronized by the Empress Dowager, the mother of the Wanli emperor, were eventually punished for alleged criticisms of the person of the emperor— the former died in prison while the other was exiled in disgrace to Guangdong province before being appointed by the state to reform the famous but decayed Nanhua Monastery. The hand of the Ming state was felt particularly in the reform of monasteries, as officials named abbots, managed monastic lands, and donated funds for restoration, as we just saw in the career of Hanshan Deqing. In blurring the distinctions between Buddhist schools, all four monks advocated a syncretistic approach in worship, combining Chan meditation with Pure Land prayer. The significance of the Buddhist laity is reflected in the large following of Confucian scholars enjoyed by Zhuhong and Zhiyu, who emphasized the harmony and compatibility between Buddhist doctrines and Confucian discourse in their writings. These developments reflected a convergence between the development of neo-Confucian thought and the rapprochement with Confucianism by Buddhist intellectuals in the Late Ming, which saw a valorization of the ideas of the 16th-century scholar-official

Wang Yangming. Wang's ideas of conscience, self-reflection, and subjective knowledge found a wide echo in Buddhist teachings, and provided an intellectual context for the Confucian reception of Buddhism. The dynamic interchange between Buddhism and Confucianism reflected a growing openness to religious and intellectual experimentation in the Late Ming. By presenting themselves as followers of a quasi-Buddhist theology, the first Jesuits to enter Ming China received a mostly friendly reception from the Buddhist clergy. Even later, after the Jesuits changed tactics (at Ricci's initiative) to present themselves as scholars rather than monks, the westerners were met with curiosity rather than hostility. Three of the four prominent monks mentioned above had either personal encounters with Ricci or were engaged in polemical exchanges—the latter only as a consequence of Ricci's fierce attacks on Buddhism.

Occupying a distinct second place to Buddhism in popularity, Daoism nevertheless flourished in the Ming dynasty thanks to strong state support. Three Ming emperors of the 15th century sponsored a comprehensive compendium of extant Daoist literature, the *Daozang* (Daoist Canon); these emperors paid for the tome's engraving, printing, and distribution to Daoist temples throughout the realm. Two emperors were particularly supportive: in the early 15th century, Yongle ordered the restoration of the temples of Mount Wudang in Hubei, one of Daoism's most sacred mountains, and in the early 16th century, the Jiaqing emperor became intensely interested in the elixirs of life and in the esoteric Daoist sexual arts for increasing vitality and health.

While the appointment of Daoist masters at the imperial court and state sponsorship of Daoist temple repairs represented the official face of Ming Daoism, at the local and popular level this indigenous Chinese religion readily blended into local folk traditions. In many practices and rituals, there was a remarkable resemblance to, or synthesis with, Buddhism. Ming religions were above all *practical*: used to avert natural disasters; to appease the spirits of ancestors, demons, or ghosts; to ask for good health and cure diseases; and to prepare for an eternal life. All Ming religions shared a belief in causality. Good works brought redemption; evil deeds caused punishments; and everyone was free to experiment with any ritual means available to gain merit and avoid punishments. Religion was a practice, and piety and virtue could be measured; nowhere was this more clearly expressed than in the many morality books and ledgers of merit and demerit available to the buyer to monitor daily spiritual progress. Prayer beads, pious donations, release of animals, keeping fasts, burning of amulets, buying signs, endowing religious services, quiet meditation, and pilgrimages—these items and services were all available for purchase in the free market of religious ideas and practices serving the men and women of Late Ming society, for whose spiritual allegiance the newcomers, the Jesuit missionaries from Europe, would have to compete.

Matteo Ricci

Matteo Ricci was born in 1552 in Macerata, a town situated in the Italian Marche, a mountainous province of the Papal States near the Adriatic and close to the famous pilgrimage site of Loreto. His father, Giovanni, a prosperous pharmacist, sent Matteo, the eldest of many children, to study with the fathers of the Society of Jesus, a new religious order known for its excellent schools. At the age of eighteen, Matteo was sent by his father to study law at La Sapienza, the university in Rome, jurisprudence being the best preparation for sons of ambitious urban families seeking to ascend the ladder of success in the papal administration. But a seed had been planted in the mind of the young Ricci by his preceptors, and after two years of legal studies, Matteo left the university to join the Jesuits.

Judging by the letters he wrote late in life, the six years Ricci spent as a Jesuit novice in Rome (1571–77) were probably the happiest in his memory. While enjoying the companionship of his *confreres* and the direction of his teachers, Ricci came to know two important men during his course of liberal arts and philosophy: the aristocrat-turned-Jesuit Alessandro Valignano (Master of novices and later Visitor of India and Japan, and twice Ricci's superior), and the German Christoph Clavius (Professor of Mathematics at the Collegio Romano of the Jesuits), with whom Ricci enjoyed a lifelong rapport. Two traits seemed to have distinguished this young Jesuit in his formative years: a love for scientific knowledge—astronomy, mathematics, geography—and a religious fervor. When, in 1576, the Portuguese Jesuit Martim da Silva came to Rome seeking recruits, Ricci petitioned to become a missionary overseas.

In May 1577, Ricci left his youthful life to enter into an unknown world. With other would-be missionaries, he traveled to Portugal where he spent the next ten months in preparation for his overseas missions, studying Portuguese and beginning theology. In March of the following year Ricci was shipped out with other missionaries, one of whom was Michele Ruggieri, a fellow Italian nine years older than Ricci and later his closest companion in China. After a difficult six-month voyage, this convoy arrived in Goa, capital of the Portuguese State of India. Ricci remained in India between September 1578 and April 1582. His first letters date from this period. They tell of a difficult period of transition. Ricci adjusted badly to tropical heat and frequently came down with fevers, one of which almost killed him. Ordained as a priest, Ricci spent two years completing his theological training while teaching Greek in the Jesuit colleges in Goa and Cochin. College life reminded Ricci of what he missed, especially the happy friendships of his years in Rome; his letters hint at a strong nostalgia for home and Italy. Nevertheless, there were things to interest and incense him in India. In the former category was the progress of Jesuit missionaries in the court of the powerful Mughal emperor Akbar; in the latter, the exclusion, at Jesuit colleges, of native converts and Indian students from theological studies. This exclusionary practice followed the Society's general policy of not admitting natives to its ranks and reflected the racial prejudice of Portuguese colonialism. Rescue from the languor of tropical heat came in the form of a letter from Valignano, who ordered Ricci to travel to Macao, there to join Ruggieri, who had left India in 1579 to prepare for a new mission.

In the first decades of its existence, the Portuguese enclave of Macao had a mixed population of a few thousand Portuguese and their servants, as well as Chinese seafarers and merchants, many from southern Fujian. While Portuguese political and ecclesiastical administrations were being established, several religious orders had already settled in this doorstep to China. The small Jesuit community comprised fewer than ten and served mainly to support the much larger and flourishing mission in Japan; Ruggieri was the only non-Portuguese member. He was also the only one who devoted himself to the serious study of the Chinese language and culture, having been charged to do so by Valignano. As traders, the Portuguese relied on Chinese middlemen and interpreters when they embarked on their twice-yearly trade fairs to Guangzhou, the provincial capital of Guangdong a half-day's sail up the Pearl River. The great majority of Portuguese clergy in this faraway enclave were there to tend to the spiritual needs of the Portuguese, their servants, and slaves, and Ruggieri's zest for conversions was considered quixotic and a waste of time. Nonetheless, this pioneer of the China mission persisted. Ruggieri learned Chinese without any primer, working toward fluency character by character with the help of an adolescent Chinese convert. For three years he labored on before help arrived in the person of his erstwhile shipmate from Portugal, the younger *confrere* Matteo Ricci.

With the firm support of Valignano, who was busy directing both the Japan and India missions while keeping his eyes on China, this handful of Jesuits—initially the three Italians Ruggieri, Ricci, and Francesco Pasio (1554–1612)—set out to establish a mission in the interior of the vast Ming Empire. Thanks to Ruggieri's linguistic abilities, however imperfect, and to his knowledge of Chinese courtesies and rituals, in 1582 he, accompanied by Pasio, gained a foothold in Zhaoqing, the site of the supreme government of the two provinces of Guangdong and Guangxi. This success was short-lived, however, because their protector, the mandarin Chen Rui, was indicted for corruption; the two Italians reluctantly left for Macao. While Pasio then departed for Japan, Ruggieri was recalled to Zhaoqing within a year, this time accompanied by Ricci.

The Jesuits had found a new protector: the mandarin Wang Pan, who had received reports of their efficacy as religious practitioners. In exchange for his protection, Wang, who was seeking a son, asked the two missionaries to don Chinese Buddhist garb, a logical consequence to Ruggieri's self-presentation as monks from India. In these early years in Zhaoqing, 1583 to 1586, this sense of mistaken identity allowed the Christian mission to survive. Dressed as Buddhist monks, the Jesuits came armed with images, doctrines, and devotions that reminded the Chinese of Buddhism: pictures of the Virgin Mary, of the Infant Jesus, the rosary beads and prayers, the teaching of heaven and hell, sin and redemption—all these would find homologies in Buddhism. In fact, Wang Pan prayed to an image of Madonna and Child, and celebrated the happy birth of a son with offerings to the foreign missionaries. Of the eighty or so converts in Zhaoqing, the great majority were formerly devout Buddhists. To what extent these converts perceived Christianity as a religion totally different from Buddhism remains an open question, given that Buddhist terms were employed frequently in the very first Chinese language Christian text, *Tianzhu shilu* (A Veritable Record of the Lord of Heaven), composed by Ruggieri with the help of his Chinese language tutor.

This overlap between Christianity and Buddhism was both a result of Chinese expectation and Ruggieri's conscious missionary policy. Unlike his younger companion, Ricci, who would develop an intense hostility toward Buddhism, Ruggieri was more accommodating: Buddhism was the most popular religion in China, hence subverting it from within seemed more workable than outright confrontation. Moreover, certain

Buddhist practices, such as vegetarianism and fasting, contributed to moral discipline. Ruggieri, the better linguist and more experienced missionary, wrote poems in classical Chinese using Buddhist terms, and enjoyed his role as a learned religious cleric patronized by mandarins. In the winter of 1585–86, Ruggieri and Antonio de Almeida (1557–91), a young Portuguese Jesuit sent from Macao, traveled from Guangzhou to Shaoxing in Zhejiang province in the entourage of Wang Pan's brother, a silk merchant who came to trade in the south. Their six-month sojourn scored only one conversion—Wang Pan's seventy-year-old father—and the Jesuits returned to Zhaoqing, where their warm relations with their patron Wang Pan suddenly cooled. This magistrate's friendship with the erudite foreign monks assumed a new liability.

Thirty years after their settlement, the Portuguese presence in Macao remained controversial. Conservative mandarins cited concerns for maritime security, and the fear of piracy, which added to an existing sense of xenophobia, was real for the inhabitants of Guangdong province. Tensions with Japan rose, culminating in the 1592 Japanese invasion of Korea and six years of Ming Chinese involvement in the resistance. Blatant association with foreigners became a liability. Meanwhile, the relationship between Ruggieri and Ricci seems to have become strained.

By 1588, Ricci had spent six years in China, five of those in Zhaoqing. He had grown from a novice missionary into a seasoned one, as his knowledge of the Chinese language and culture began to equal, and eventually surpassed, that of his senior colleague. Ricci was finding his own way as a missionary. His way differed significantly from Ruggieri's in that Ricci could appeal to the Chinese elites with his scientific knowledge and interest. Long before Ricci had acquired enough linguistic expertise to compose his first Chinese text, he had adapted for display a universal world map made by the Belgian cartographer Abraham Ortelius. With Latin terms and explanations translated into Chinese, this large wall map was displayed prominently in the Jesuits' house together with prisms, crystals, clocks, western books, and other items that made the residence a curiosity cabinet for the many mandarins whose official visits to the Supreme Commander of Guangdong and Guangxi brought them to town. Ricci impressed his Chinese visitors with his knowledge of cartography, geography, mechanics, and mathematics; he also hinted at his interest in Chinese culture, asking for copies of poems by visitors and revealing his studies in the Confucian Canon, the *Four Books* and *Five Classics* (all of which, you will recall, formed the basis of education and the civil service examination in Late Imperial China). During these years Ricci developed a strong disagreement with Ruggieri's conversion methods: to Ricci's mind, there was nothing in common between Christianity and Buddhism. In fact, the latter religion was the chief obstacle to evangelization. The role of Buddhist clergy, projected onto the Jesuits by their Chinese patrons, began to irritate Ricci ever more.

Frustrated by their slow progress in evangelization, Ruggieri decided in 1588 to take a bold step: he would return to Rome to ask for a papal diplomatic mission to the Ming capital. Behind his back, Valignano, the Visitor in Macao, and Ricci, now the senior missionary in Zhaoqing, exchanged correspondence in which they expressed doubts about Ruggieri's future in the China mission: he was too timid, his spoken Chinese too poor, he was too old; he had served his purpose and should not be returned to China should a papal legation materialize. In November 1588, Ruggieri left Macao for Europe. Though the papacy was interested in his plea, it was too involved in European affairs to act on his proposal. Retiring to Naples, Ruggieri died in 1607, leaving behind a manuscript full of reminiscences of his years in China.

Meanwhile, Ricci met with his own setbacks. In May 1589, the new Supreme Commander Liu Jiezhai requisitioned the Jesuit residence, offering the missionaries a choice of returning to Macao or relocating to a more remote place in Guangdong, far from the centers of power and attention. Ricci, forced to abandon the eighty-strong Christian community in Zhaoqing, left for Shaozhou in northern Guangdong—a provincial town with a famous Buddhist monastery—accompanied by Almeida, two Chinese Jesuit brothers, and several servants.

Ricci spent six years in Shaozhou (1589–95). These were years of setbacks, but also of achievements that gave Ricci the chance for a breakthrough. In terms of obstacles, Ricci found himself in a provincial backwater, albeit one situated on the major line of communication between Guangdong and the provinces to the north. The illnesses and subsequent deaths of two of his companions—the young Almeida and his successor, the Italian Francesco de Petris—deeply affected Ricci. His letters from these years reflect a profound loneliness, accentuated by news of the death of the grandmother who had raised him back in Macerata. Stress added to depression when the Jesuits ran afoul of hostile young men in the neighborhood, who broke into the residence one night, an incident during which Ricci seriously injured his foot. Fortunately for Ricci, he enjoyed the protection and favor of the local magistrates, thanks to the extensive network that he had patiently built up in Zhaoqing and to his own charisma, which attracted a new disciple, one who would become his friend for life.

Qu Rukui (literary name Taisu) was the black sheep of a very prominent family in Changshu in Jiangsu province, the richest region of China. A wanderer, Qu first met Ricci in Zhaoqing and was immediately struck by the westerner's personality and looks. Mistaking Ricci to be a master of hidden arts, including alchemy, Qu sought out Ricci in Shaozhou and, when disabused of his first ideas, became an avid student of mathematics and Christian doctrines. Using Qu's connections, Ricci gained access to the regional mandarins' inner circle. Of the few converts he still made, most were merchant sojourners from northern provinces who seemed to possess a spiritual quality and religious interest not previously experienced by Ricci. Abandoning the Buddhist approach, Ricci rejected the *Tianzhu shilu*—the catechism composed by Ruggieri—and began a new work. On the advice of Qu, who explained the low social status and generally poor intellectual level of the Buddhist clergy, Ricci decided to cast off the Buddhist persona and adopt the role of a Confucian scholar working within the Jesuit order. Valignano approved the change in tactics, which required an entirely new look for Ricci. Dressed in black silk, with a full length of hair and long beard, Ricci could now pretend to be the social equal of the Chinese elites.

Ricci was well aware that a change of clothing alone would fail to impress the Chinese elites. He needed to study their books. Resuming an intensive course in the Confucian classics, Ricci began to translate them into Latin, a project that was passed on to future generations of Jesuits and came to fruition only two generations after his death. Ricci's education in the humanities prepared him well for this task. His analytical mind was aided enormously by his stunning memory. His background in Latin and Greek primed Ricci for more than just the study of classical Chinese texts. Inspired by his deep understanding of the history and cultures of ancient Greece and Rome, Ricci realized a vision for the evangelization of China: just as early western Christianity grew out of Greek philosophy and adopted Latin and Greek as its ecclesiastical languages, so Christianity in China could grow in conversation with Confucian philosophy.

In the spring of 1595, just when Ricci was intellectually and psychologically prepared for a new stage in his work, he was suddenly offered the chance to accompany a high-ranking mandarin on a trip to Beijing.

The invitation was a godsend. This mandarin had sought out the Jesuits because his son was suffering from depression, having failed in a recent imperial civil service examination. As a result of Ruggieri's experience counseling a member of the Wang family clan in the winter of 1586, the westerners had gained a reputation as psychic healers. After following Ruggieri's earlier route through the pass at Meiling hills and the Gan River in Jiangxi, Ricci parted ways with his mandarin patron in Nanchang, the provincial capital. It was decided that Ricci would not go to Beijing after all, but head to Nanjing instead.

The primary capital during the first two reigns of the Ming dynasty, Nanjing remained the second capital of the realm, equipped with a smaller version of Beijing's Forbidden City and a skeleton bureaucracy. Although little real political power was centered there, Nanjing was at the center of Jiangnan, a region of dense urban networks, economically the richest and culturally the most advanced province in Ming China. At the end of May 1595, Ricci, full of hopes, arrived in this magnificent city. He paid a visit to Xu Daren, a mandarin acquaintance from his Zhaoqing days. Shocked and surprised by Ricci's appearance, Xu treated the Jesuit rudely and sent him away, for Ming China was at war with Japan and Xu feared guilt by association with a foreigner. A dejected Ricci returned to Nanchang, where in two short years he would make yet another breakthrough in his career.

The trip to Beijing that Ricci envisioned—a journey that would take him from the southern coastline of China to its capital in the far north—was finally made possible by his gradual ascent on the ladder of success in Late Ming society. In Nanchang, Ricci mingled not only with mandarins but also with princes of the imperial line. After the early 15th century, the Ming regime devised a system to prevent lesser princes of the imperial line from wielding political influence in the capital by granting them parcels of land in the provinces. Endowed with mini-palaces, land, and a staff, princes of imperial blood settled like a layer of privilege and consumption over the vast realm of taxpayers. The number of these provincial princes multiplied with every generation until, in the 17th century, they consumed a considerable part of the state's budget. Deprived of any political power, they formed an elite leisure class. Ricci dedicated his very first Chinese work—*Jiaoyou lun* (On Friendship), a short work in which maxims on the subject from Greco-Roman texts were juxtaposed with quotations from the Confucian classics—to one of these princes in Nanchang. A second work, *Xiguo jifa* (The Art of Memory of the West), owed its composition to Chinese scholars' incredulous reactions to Ricci's prodigious memory and their incessant demand that he teach them this arcane art, which they viewed as a secret path to success in the imperial service examination.

Acting as the senior Jesuit of the China mission, Ricci maintained communication with Shaozhou and Macao, bringing in missionary reinforcements and supplies. His brilliant displays of his mathematical, astronomical, and scientific knowledge continued to expand his reputation among the Chinese elites. As he mounted the rungs of Ming society, Ricci became more captivated by its cultural achievements. He wrote at length on the system of government, which was manned by magistrates schooled in Confucian texts and selected through the imperial civil service examination. He also engaged in an intense dialogue with Zhang Huang (1527–1608), the leading Confucian scholar in Nanchang and director of a famous academy that dated back to the neo-Confucianist days of the Song dynasty. Although they held different views on the existence of heaven and hell (Zhang Huang was an agnostic), both men agreed that virtue was the highest goal of public life and the source of good governance and social discipline. Through Zhang Huang and his own intense study of Confucian texts, Ricci came to view Confucianism, the dominant school of thought in Late Imperial China, as promoting a worldview similar to that advanced by stoicism, the early Greek philosophy espoused by, for example, Epictetus, the 1st-century Greek thinker who was eventually honored by Christians. Likewise, through his conversations with Zhang Huang, Ricci understood how key passages in the *Four Books* and *Five Classics* could be harmonized with Christian social ethics, and could possibly be interpreted to accommodate a Christian message of revelation and redemption. A conversion strategy, based on a Christian-Confucian synthesis, was slowly taking shape in Ricci's mind.

In June 1598 another opportunity knocked on Ricci's door. The mandarin Wang Zhongming, who had previously met Ricci in Shaozhou, was traveling from his native home in Ding'an in Hainan to Beijing. Passing through Nanchang, he promised to take Ricci with him. Hastily departing with the Italian Jesuit Lazaro Cattaneo (1560–1640) and a Chinese Jesuit brother, Ricci embarked for the next stage in his quest.

After a brief stay in Nanjing, Minister Wang and the Jesuits sailed on the Grand Canal for Beijing. Ricci finally arrived at the imperial capital in September 1598. He was, however, still a man of no significance. Unable to make any connections with the powerful, Ricci left after two months. Disappointed and exhausted, Ricci returned to Jiangnan to visit his friend Qu Taisu, who advised him to settle in Nanjing.

Ricci spent only fifteen months in the southern capital after arriving there in February 1599. Yet this was a crucial period for him. As the center of cultural life during the Ming dynasty, Nanjing offered Ricci a more exalted and wider circle of contacts. The city's imperial observatory, with instruments dating back to the 14th century, deeply impressed Ricci; he found new admirers and friends among the large number of mandarins and scholars living there; and he practiced his Jesuit polemics for the first time on Nanjing's Buddhist intellectuals, both lay and clerical.

Nanjing made Ricci's career. Among the mandarin acquaintances he made, several were later promoted to higher ranks in Beijing, and one, Ye Xianggao (1559–1627), became patron to a later generation of Jesuit missionaries. Ricci attracted admirers and students from the many scholars he met, men eager to learn western methods of mathematics and astronomy. Even those who disapproved of his anti-Buddhist discourses found him a remarkable and interesting man, worthy of their time and attention. Li Zhi (1527–1602), a Buddhist layman, ex-mandarin, and the most famous nonconformist in the Late Ming, was among Ricci's many admirers. Still others were fascinated by Ricci's printed books, paintings, clocks, and astronomical instruments. Ricci basked in all this attention, which only sharpened his combativeness toward Buddhism.

At a banquet in Nanjing, Ricci entered into a long and acerbic debate with Abbot Xuelang Hong'en (d. 1607), the leading Buddhist cleric in Nanjing, whose erudition and personality had earned him an excellent reputation among the literati. This confrontation represented a catharsis for Ricci, who, as we recall, adopted the public image of a western Buddhist monk during his first years in China. The trials and tribulations of those early eleven years (1583–94)—when the role of a Buddhist monk had required that he shave his hair and beard and don a garment signifying social inferiority—still rankled Ricci. Ricci's new Confucian persona liberated him; and intellectual engagement with Confucianism formed the missionary's mental arsenal in a new conversion strategy. Henceforth, Ricci would use aspects of Confucian teachings to refute Buddhism; he would advance the cause of Christianity by arguing for the harmony and synergy between the western faith and Chinese philosophy; and, by demonstrating the superiority of western science and logic, he would bring Confucian elites to embrace the mysteries of the Christian faith.

Buoyed by success, Ricci again planned for another visit to Beijing. This time he would go in the capacity of an unofficial envoy bearing gifts from Europe—a clavichord, western clocks, paintings, books, and prisms—brought to China from Macao in March 1600 by the Spanish Jesuit Diego da Pantoja. With the help of sympathetic mandarins, Ricci equipped another expedition and set out on the Grand Canal once more with Pantoja in May. Along the leisurely boat trip, the Jesuits experienced firsthand the dark side of Late Ming politics. Tired of administering his vast empire and distrustful of his mandarins, Emperor Wanli (reign 1573–1620) conceded enormous power to his palace eunuchs. Many of these eunuchs held important posts as tax collectors and customs officials, including one Ma Tang who, hoping to exact bribery as an intermediary, intercepted the Jesuits on the Grand Canal. When Ricci's memorial to the imperial court received no reply, the Jesuits were placed effectively under house arrest. During a search of their baggage, Ma Tang confronted Ricci with a crucifix he had found, thinking it an instrument of magic. Between July 1600 and January 1601, Ricci and Pantoja were unwilling "guests" of the avaricious eunuch before an edict finally arrived summoning the Europeans to court.

Although Ricci was not granted an imperial audience, the western gifts, especially the clavichord and the clock, intrigued the emperor. The Jesuits were allowed to stay and a stipend was granted for their livelihood. Beijing was to be Ricci's last home. In time, the Jesuits purchased a residence outside the Inner City near the Xuanwu Gate, where they built a church and a residence. Ricci made many powerful friends. But few were numbered among the converts, whose number grew in nine years to almost one thousand. Of Ricci's Chinese friends and associates, two were especially important: Xu Guangqi (1562–1633) and Li Zhizao (1565–1630). Both were middle-rank mandarins in these years, although Xu would rise to the highest mandarin rank two decades after Ricci's death. A native of Shanghai, Xu first met Ricci in Nanjing. Like many of his peers, Xu was initially attracted by Ricci's reputation as a great scholar in mathematics; unlike most of them, Xu, a devout Buddhist at one point in his life, sought spiritual fulfillment. Inspired by a religious dream, Xu received catechism in Nanjing after Ricci's departure and became the westerner's greatest collaborator and admirer in Beijing. Li Zhizao was likewise attracted by Ricci's knowledge of theoretical and applied sciences. Like Xu, he also collaborated closely with Ricci, but only converted a short time before Ricci's death in 1610. Thanks to his collaboration with Xu and Li, Ricci's Beijing years were intellectually the most productive period of his life.

As we recall, Ricci was already a successful author in Nanchang, having published popular short works on friendship and western mnemonics. The World Map he had displayed in Zhaoqing proved to be an even more enduring success, and was reprinted several times (without his knowledge) by Chinese scholars; an expanded version of this map was now presented to the Wanli emperor. During his Beijing years Ricci added another dozen texts to his body of work, some of which were published while some remained manuscripts. These later works can be divided into three categories. First, there were two occasional short texts on western culture; Chinese songs with Christian themes, composed for performance on the clavichord and offered to the emperor; and a booklet to the son of a friend, *Xizi qiji* (Miracle of Western Letters), with explanations for biblical illustrations written in Chinese characters and annotated with their sounds in the Latin alphabet. A second category, the largest, comprised scientific works. Ricci collaborated with Xu and Li on these works, which ranged from translations and guides to astronomy to texts on theoretical and applied mathematics. Ricci would dictate the texts while his Chinese friends took notes and supplied technical terms in Chinese. Ricci translated three mathematical works into Chinese: the first two books of Euclid's *Geometry*, and two adaptations of works by Clavius, his professor in Rome, the *Epitome Arithmeticae Practicae* (Summary of Applied Mathematics) and a work on linear algebra and plane geometry. Ricci's chief astronomical work is *Qiankun tiyi* (On the Nature of the Cosmos), which includes explanations of Ptolemaic cosmology—which placed the earth at the center of nine concentric spheres with fixed stars—and demonstrations of measurements and calculations showing the solar and lunar eclipses. The celestial sphere, the chief instrument for stargazing, is explained in this work as well as in a general work on astronomical instruments; and finally there is a manuscript with star maps, explanations of eclipses, and geometric figures. The third and final category comprised Ricci's philosophical and theological writings. These represented Ricci's most original work and summed up his career in the China mission.

Tianzhu shiyi (True Meaning of the Lord of Heaven) is Ricci's most important work. Though he began work on the *Tianzhu shiyi*—which he intended as a replacement for Ruggieri's own introduction to Christianity (the *Tianzhu shilu*)—while he was in Shaozhou, Ricci did not finish this book until more than a decade later in 1603. The long period of gestation and completion reflected Ricci's evolving dialogue with Chinese culture, particularly with Confucianism and Buddhism, and assumed its final form only after he had adopted the strategy of a Confucian-Christian alliance against Buddhism. In *Tianzhu shiyi*, there are echoes of the conversations between Ricci and Zhang Huang in Nanchang, dialogues between the Jesuit and his other Chinese friends over the years, and perhaps repetitions of the angry arguments he had with Abbot Xuelang Hong'en in Nanjing. Cast in the form of a dialogue between a western and a Chinese scholar, the book consists of eight chapters divided into two parts. In chapters 1 to 4, Ricci uses natural philosophy to demonstrate Christian theology. The Lord of Heaven, the Christian God, is the creator and provider of all things, who has not been properly acknowledged by all men. In his creation mankind stands at the apex, for human beings alone possess a soul distinct from animals. The nobility of the human soul also differentiates him from demons and angels, and it is a fallacy to assert that all things in nature make up one unified substance. In these chapters, Ricci cites passages from the Confucian Canon, especially from the *Book of History* and *Book of Poetry*, that name an Emperor on High (*Shangdi*); Ricci equates this emperor with the Christian God. The true God, therefore, was known already by the ancient Chinese, implying that Christianity was by no means a completely alien cultural import. To bolster his argument, Ricci employs natural philosophy to demonstrate the necessary existence of a creator, playing to his own reputation as a great mathematician and astronomer. In arguing for the uniqueness of the human soul and against the unitary substance of the universe, Ricci refutes key teachings in Buddhism and in neo-Confucianism.

Turning next to a direct attack, Ricci ridicules the Buddhist teaching of reincarnation and karma, and dismisses the idea of non-killing and vegetarianism. Countering the materialistic philosophy of neo-Confucianism, Ricci maintains the existence of heaven and hell, life after death, and the rewards of virtue and evil. Christian ethics is not so different from Confucianism in that it advocates the original goodness of man, striking a common chord with the teachings of the Confucian sage Mencius. Like Confucianism, Christianity—which he rendered as "the Learning of Heaven" in Chinese—is orthodox. Right doctrines lead to right beliefs and correct behavior, as Ricci explains how the Catholic clergy, embracing celibacy in their single-minded quest for true learning, brings these doctrines to the whole world. The book ends with a short narrative of the birth of Christ in Judea.

Jiren shipian (Ten Discourses of the Man of Paradox), published in 1608, is a work that equals *Tianzhu shiyi* in importance, if not in fame. In the book, Ricci discourses on the brevity of life, the imminence of death, preparations for a good end, the virtue of silence, the correct reasons for fasting, self-reflection and the examination of conscience, the reward of virtue and punishment of evil after death, the vanity of fortune-telling, and the burden of material wealth. The significance of these discourses lies not in their originality, for they deal with conventional themes in Christian philosophy, but rather in their context: they name real interlocutors—including Xu Guangqi, Li Zhizao, and Merchant Guo, an elderly but fervent convert in Ricci's Shaozhou days—and contain the kernel of actual conversations that Ricci must have had with his Chinese counterparts. In this work, art and memory collaborate to create a work vivid in the immediacy of dialogue between the western missionary and actual Chinese personages.

By contrast, *Ershiwu yan* (The Twenty-Five *Sententiae*), probably written in 1599 and published in 1602, is a less original work. It consists of adapted excerpts from Epictetus' *Encheiridion*. But as an introduction of Stoic philosophy to Ming China, it was immensely successful. Its publication was sponsored by Feng Yingjing, a prominent and righteous mandarin imprisoned for daring to oppose corrupt and violent eunuchs, minions of the Wanli emperor. To live in equanimity in an age of injustice and tyranny, such was the lesson of Epictetus. Chinese readers of *Ershiwu yan* would not know about the life of Epictetus (whose name is not mentioned in the book), during which the majority of Roman emperors were either poisoned or assassinated, and one of whom, Nero, forced his tutor, the great Stoic philosopher Seneca, to commit suicide. They would, however, find in the book reflections of many of the same issues plaguing their own times: the impotence of the emperor, his neglect of state affairs, the prevalence of official corruption, and the rapacity and cruelty of palace eunuchs—trusted minions of a man neglectful of the well-being of his subjects and of the political ethics of a Confucian ruler.

The final work is a long letter in reply to Yu Chunxi. A mandarin and devout lay Buddhist, Yu resented Ricci's attacks on Buddhism. In exquisitely polite and elegant prose, he wrote an open letter faulting Ricci for ignorance and narrow-mindedness and inviting him to a closer study of the Buddhist sutras. Responding to this literary challenge, Ricci (most likely with the help of Xu Guangqi) composed an equally elegant letter defending the teachings of Christianity and denigrating those of Buddhism. This was the first literary barrage in the war between Christianity and Buddhism, a conflict that would last for another fifty years in 17th-century China.

In Beijing, Ricci spurned the approach of a famous Buddhist monk and rejoiced in any setbacks dealt to this supposedly "rival" religion. If the Catholic Church could fight Protestant "heretics" in Europe, her sons in the China mission would fight Buddhism. Toward another religious community Ricci showed more curiosity than hostility. Notice came to him of the remains of a once flourishing Jewish community in Kaifeng in Henan province, and Ricci dispatched a Chinese Jesuit lay brother to visit. Toward Muslims and Daoists Ricci manifested little interest; only the Confucian scholars attracted his full attention, for in their conversion, Ricci reasoned, was the future of Christianity in China, and it was in competition for their spiritual allegiance that war must be declared on Buddhism.

After many years of travel, Ricci finally came to rest in Beijing. The world was now coming to him. A frequent guest at the tables of the powerful and learned, Ricci kept a very busy social schedule and carefully cultivated a vast network of connections in the mandarin world. Many magistrates and scholars arriving in the capital visited the Jesuit compound to see its books, clocks, and astronomical instruments, to gaze at paintings and statues of the Virgin Mary and Christ, and to converse with the great man, the remarkable western scholar, who was so steeped in Chinese culture that, aside from his countenance, he seemed to be one of them. On top of this unrelenting social schedule, Ricci directed the growing Christian community and his small group of Jesuits and servants. He lectured, said mass, administered sacraments, and answered correspondence, all the while producing his impressive body of works. In 1608, at the age of fifty-six, Ricci felt tired and old. Overtaken by nostalgia, he began to write down in detail his story, set in the context of the introduction of Christianity in China. Calling up in his prodigious memory events and persons past and present, Ricci had not finished his manuscript before he fell ill and died on May 11, 1610.

By the time of his death Ricci had become a celebrity. Many came to the Jesuit residence to pay last respects at his wake. The request of his mandarin friends for an official funeral was granted by the emperor. Conceded a few times in the Early Ming to foreign princes and envoys on tribute-bearing missions in China, a state-sponsored funeral represented a signal honor. A plot of land to the west of the walled city was set aside for this purpose. The Jesuits built a chapel and Ricci was laid to rest more than a year later, the first of many western Jesuit missionaries who would be buried there in the following centuries.

In Europe, Ricci's success became legendary. In Rome, some talked excitedly of the Chinese emperor's imminent conversion to Christianity. Replying, in his last letters, to all this adulation, Ricci was clear-eyed about the modest harvest of souls he had reaped in his lifetime. The China mission represented merely a young seedling, Ricci admonished, which needed to be protected against adversity. But better a few high-quality converts than massive baptisms, for those elites—men like Xu and Li— would provide protection against contrary winds. Nonetheless, Ricci's remarkable career was a spectacular success. That success meant even more to Catholic Europe and the Society of Jesus as the mission in Japan was running into a violent storm: in 1598, the new hegemon Hideyoshi executed the first Christians, both Japanese and European. His successor Tokugawa Ieyasu, who came to power in 1600, showed little sympathy for Christianity and banned it a few years after Ricci's death, expelling all foreign missionaries and forbidding Portuguese merchants to set foot on Japanese soil. Those missionaries who remained were hunted down mercilessly and executed, together with thousands of Japanese martyrs. In this larger context of missionary history, the memory of Ricci and the future success of the Jesuit mission in China loomed ever larger.

In 1611, the Belgian Jesuit Nicolas Trigault arrived in Beijing. Four years later he returned to Europe to raise funds and recruits for the China mission, bringing with him the unfinished manuscript of Ricci's memoirs. Translating it from Italian into Latin and editing it into a seamless narrative, Trigault published *De Christiana expeditione apud Sinas* (The Christian Expedition to China) in 1615. It was well and widely received. In public opinion, Ricci stood on equal terms with Francis Xavier, among Ignatius' first companions and the first Jesuit missionary in Asia, canonized together with the Society's founder in 1622 and venerated as the patron of Catholic missions. Ricci's legacy ensured that there would be no shortage of Jesuit missionaries in the 250 years after his death. The tender seedling he planted grew into a sturdy tree that withstood the repeated storms of persecutions. Perspicacious in his vision, Ricci was right that elite converts—men such as Xu Guangqi—would protect and nourish the growing Christian community. By accommodating himself to Chinese culture,

Ricci enabled Christians in the Late Ming and the Early Qing dynasties to express their own understanding of this foreign religion in a synthesis of Chinese learning and western doctrines. Even in hard times for the missionaries and Chinese converts—whether during the suppression of the Jesuit order in 1773 or the persecutions in 1784—Ricci's legacy would endure. After the mid-19th century, when Christianity was again declared legal in China after the prohibition in 1705, the memory of Ricci became poignant for the Chinese. Faced with a new missionary culture, formed by European imperialist arrogance and protected by colonial privileges, Christianity in China had to overcome the antagonism between nationalism and racism and looked back with nostalgia to a bygone golden age.

Ricci in Our Time

On January 10, 2014, the Congregation for the Causes of Saints in Rome received the dossiers on Matteo Ricci's beatification. Thus began a familiar process, standardized in the early 17th century, where individuals who had lived their lives heroically according to the theological virtues of the Catholic Church may eventually be proclaimed beatified and canonized. A Relator would be appointed by the Vatican to collect and examine the records related to the candidate's claim to sainthood.

In making saints, the Roman Catholic Church relies on documents to pronounce on the character of an individual in the past, not unlike the work of historians. What is indeed the significance of Matteo Ricci for our time?

We know what it may mean for the Vatican. Monsignor Giuliodori, the bishop of Macerata, a major sponsor behind this move, alluded to the implications that the news about the progress made in the sainthood cause would have for the Holy See's relations with China: "I hope that with Pope Francis' input there will be a push in the direction of evangelization and dialogue with China," he said. Despite several negotiations in recent years, China and the Vatican failed to reestablish diplomatic ties, which were cut in 1950, when the victorious Communists expelled all western missionaries from the country. The history of Christianity in East Asia has a resonance that goes far beyond Ricci's death.

Indeed, Ricci's cause now rests with the first Jesuit pope in the history of Roman Catholicism, a pope who visited South Korea in mid-August 2014 and declared 124 Korean Christian martyrs "blessed"—the first step toward possible sainthood—to the great cheer of the Korean Catholic community. These martyrs were the early Catholic converts executed in the 18th and 19th centuries by the Joseon dynasty (1392–1910), which considered Christianity an alien, deviant, and pernicious sect. Unlike conversions in early modern China, Japan, Vietnam, or the Philippines, Christianity was introduced into Korea not by western missionaries but by a book: *The True Meaning of the Lord of Heaven* (*Tianzhu shiyi*) by Matteo Ricci.

A tribute-bearing or vassal state to Ming China, Joseon Korea imitated many aspects of Chinese civilization: it adopted Chinese writing, a similar imperial bureaucracy, and the examination system based on the study of the Confucian classics. Educated Koreans wrote in classical Chinese, and envoys visited Beijing in annual diplomatic missions. It was there that Koreans came to read Ricci's famous writing and carried his name and the text back to their native land. Admired for his synthesis of Confucian teachings and a new (Christian) ethics, Ricci's ideas were influential among a small coterie of elites until the late 18th century, when a Chinese Catholic missionary was smuggled into the country and baptized the first converts. Playing the role of founding father, the Korean nobleman Paul Yun Ji-Chung (1759–91), beyond sharing a distinction with his Chinese counterpart, Paul Xu Guangqi, who lived in a previous century, also paid for his conversion with his life. The 124 Koreans martyrs honored by Pope Francis were the most prominent of the thousands who died for their faith during the 18th and 19th centuries.

In persecuting Christianity, Joseon Korea was taking a cue from China. When Ricci died in 1610, he bequeathed a small but prospering mission to a new generation of Jesuits arriving from Europe. But in the centennial and bicentennial of his death, there would be little to cheer for the would-be saint in heaven. In 1710, Emperor Kangxi of the Manchu Qing dynasty (1644–1911), a generous patron of the Jesuits, had just issued an edict forbidding his subjects to practice Christianity. After a period of steady growth in the 17th century, Christianity in China survived the midcentury crisis of peasant uprisings and Manchu conquests; and despite some setbacks, it flourished under the reign of Kangxi (1662–1722), who admired the Jesuits for their scientific knowledge and their upright morality. The emperor was pleased with his Jesuit servants. Rather, the edict prohibiting Christian conversion in 1705 resulted from a conflict with Rome. When Spanish missionaries from the Philippines entered China in the 1630s, a generation after the death of Ricci, they questioned the conversion methods of the Jesuits. Rivalry between religious orders playing its part, the Dominicans and Franciscans criticized in particular Ricci's accommodations with Confucianism and Chinese moral practices, and complained to Rome that the Jesuits were tolerating Chinese superstitions—namely the rituals honoring departed ancestors and Confucius—which amounted to idolatry, according to the friars. The Chinese Rites Controversy, as it came to be called, was resolved against the Jesuits after bitter polemics. A papal legate was sent to China in 1705 to explain Rome's policy. Emperor Kangxi was furious at this foreign intervention in Chinese customs, based on an ill-informed understanding of Chinese texts and practices, and proclaimed new rules in 1705. Although the emperor forbade his subjects to practice Christianity, he continued to favor the Jesuits, allowing them free religious worship, but on the condition that they did not return to Europe and that they adhered "to the methods of Father Ricci."

The bicentennial of his death would have been sadder still for Ricci. In 1810, the Society of Jesus ceased to exist, except for a small community in Russia. Never without enemies within the Catholic Church, the Jesuits came under increasing criticism in the 18th century and the Society was dissolved in 1773 by Pope Clement XIV. Protected in Qing China, the ex-Jesuit missionaries were not repatriated back to Europe (unlike their fellow missionaries in Latin America, India, and Macao), sometimes to face long prison sentences. One by one, they died of old age. In 1810, only two men were left in Beijing, and Louis Poirot, the last Jesuit missionary of the old Society, lived to 1813. By the time the Society was restored in 1814, all ex-Jesuits in China had died.

On the 300th anniversary of Ricci's death, contrary winds were blowing over the Catholic Church in China. In 1910, western missionaries had returned to China, after the Qing Empire had been defeated by Britain and France in the two Opium Wars (1839–42, 1858–60) and was forced to open her territory to Christian missions. Under the protection of France, Jesuit missionaries from the restored Society returned to China and established their headquarters in Shanghai, the hometown of Paul Guangqi Xu, whose descendants had continued to adhere to the faith of their ancestors. This restored Christian mission, however, came on the heels of Chinese defeat, and rested on the diplomatic and military protection of France, one of the leading imperial powers in Asia, which saw the Catholic enterprise as an extension of national prestige. Imperialism, colonialism, and racialism strongly colored 19th-century Christian missions. In China, this provoked a violent anti-Christian movement that erupted in 1899–1900, the Boxer Uprising, that cost the lives of dozens of westerners, hundreds of Chinese converts, and thousands of peasant rebels.

Shocked by this rage against Christianity, Rome eventually steered a new course: by adopting a policy of domesticating Christianity, by training more Chinese priests, and giving greater voice to Chinese sensibilities and Chinese Catholics, the Vatican hoped to diminish the antagonism between Chinese nationalism and Christianity. In line with this new turn, the 300th anniversary of Ricci's death inspired the first effort to commemorate the missionary's great cultural achievements. In his hometown Macerata, the celebrations were jointly held by the Church and by the National Society of Geographers. The kingdom of Italy, a latecomer in the field of European imperialism and colonialism, saw Catholicism as potential soft power in its competition with stronger states such as France, Germany, and Britain, with their larger navies and armies. By celebrating Ricci, Italy drew memory to its own pioneering role in Sino-western relations. In time, this commemoration produced the first critical scholarship on Ricci: editions of his letters and writings were published; and the study of the Jesuit China mission gave an additional impetus to European sinology.

Ricci came to symbolize an alternative to the unequal status between China, dubbed "the Sick Man of the East," and the aggressive western powers. For Chinese Christians, his memory recalled a happier time of cultural dialogue based on equality, when religious conversion was not linked with western imperialist expansion. It was an uphill battle. A minority of western missionaries fought their own church and governments against discrimination and racial prejudice. One of the most prominent, the Franco-Belgian missionary Vincent Lebbe (1877–1940), a Lazarist, repeatedly confronted his superiors and French diplomats on behalf of the Chinese. The people of Tianjin, where Lebbe worked in the 1920s, called him "a second Ricci." Eventually, Lebbe took Chinese citizenship and died during the war of resistance against Japan, completing a life of perfect identification with his missionary land.

In 1949, the Communists established a new regime after their victories in the Civil War against the Nationalists, who retreated to the island of Taiwan. Borne by the force of social revolution and nationalism, the new government expelled all western missionaries. All religions were subject to party control. For Catholics, it implied cutting off ties with the

Vatican and supporting a new Patriotic Catholic Church of China. Many refused. Persecutions followed as the new regime sought to cleanse Chinese society of all vestiges of the old, climaxing in the violence of the Cultural Revolution (1966–76), when all religious buildings were closed and all worship came under attack, save for the quasi-religious adulation of Chairman Mao. With the end of the Maoist era and the inauguration of economic reforms, religious life returned to normal. Still, the question of control remained. To whom do Catholics owe their allegiance? With official ties broken, Catholicism in China is divided between the unofficial Catholic Church and the Patriotic Church. The Chinese government names all Catholic bishops and refuses to recognize those nominated by Rome. Frozen in this stalemate, the symbol of Ricci seems like a good cause to break the diplomatic ice. In 2010, during the World Exposition held in Shanghai, attended by millions of visitors, a large statue of Ricci was erected in front of the Italian pavilion. In the same year, the Ricci–Xu Guangqi Institute for the study of Sino-western relations was founded at Fudan University, one of the leading institutions of higher education and the most prominent in Shanghai. With the beginning of beatification in January 2014, Ricci is invoked again as a symbol in the hope for closer and more amicable ties between Christianity and China. Only the future will tell whether Sino-Vatican diplomatic relations come first or Ricci's sainthood. Perhaps the Jesuit missionary will only earn his wings if he can deliver this miracle.

Document 1

Excerpt from the chronicle of a Carthusian monk in Cologne, 1535.[1]

For the Catholics in Germany, the year 1535 seemed a particularly dark moment. Support for the reformer Martin Luther was growing year by year, and the tide against the Roman papacy reached a high mark in the millenarian kingdom of the Anabaptists in Münster. In nearby Cologne, Theodor Loher, a Catholic monk, reflected on the ongoing religious crisis in Europe and drew consolation from Catholic missions in the non-European world.

When Greece was involved in various heresies, finally became schismatic, and hence was cast away by God, it fell into the hands of the Muslims.... Did, therefore, the faith or the Church perish? To be sure, it has perished with those in the Orient, but meanwhile in the Occident it has increased and remained. Even if here in the Occident—on account of our sins—faith, obedience, and finally the holy sacrifice have been taken away from many cities and territories, they nevertheless remain healthy and unimpaired with others.... The kingdom is taken away from you and will be given to peoples producing his fruits. How wonderful that his Church will be constituted and will continue, after God had withdrawn it from the Jews after many blessings on account of their ingratitude and rebellion and had given it to the Gentiles, and who, now on account of the recent sins of the Christians, miraculously relinquishes them to be tainted by all manner of dissent, sects, and heresies, and lets them bite one another and be consumed and cleansed, and gives it verily to these new peoples, who have received it with the greatest desire and cherish it with love and warmth. For God is able to arouse other sons of Abraham even in the most distant nations.... But

---

1. Source: *Dionysius Carthusianus Opera Omnia*, adapted and translated from Sigrun Haude, *In the Shadow of "Savage Wolves": Anabaptist Münster and the German Reformation during the 1530s* (Boston: Humanities, 2000), pp. 67–68.

why do we say God can do this, since we know that the same is just now happening in America, Cuba, New Spain, and in other regions, populations, and languages of Great Asia through the Spaniards, and what is happening in Ethiopia, Arabia, Persia, India, and on the surrounding southern isles through the Portuguese.

Document 2

Policy debate on maritime trade among Ming officials ca. 1564.[2]

The Ming policy forbidding maritime voyages established at the beginning of the dynasty (1368) was reversed during the reign of Emperor Yongle and his son Xuande with the seven state-sponsored voyages commanded by Zheng He between 1405 and 1433. China's contact with the countries of East, South, and Southeast Asia was institutionalized in the tribute-bearing system, which regulated international commerce. By the late 15th century, a vigorous private trade developed alongside the tribute-bearing system; seafarers from southern Fujian province dominated maritime trade, more or less with official tolerance. In 1523, an act of violence committed by the Japanese tribute-bearing mission in Ningbo shocked the Ming court into reversing its maritime policy. The government shut down official state tribute missions and banned maritime commerce. Effectively driving merchants into piracy, this policy was largely responsible for the endemic Sino-Japanese pirate raids on the Chinese coast during the next four decades. In 1564, sixteen years after the successful destruction of the major pirate base at Shuangyu off the coast of Ningbo, a nest for Chinese, Japanese, and Portuguese pirates and privateers, a space for policy debate opened up. Three different views toward maritime commerce were voiced in the memorials below, submitted by three Ming officials. These ranged from maintaining the status quo of strict prohibition to an opening of maritime traffic.

Gui Youguang

Some argue that we ought to relax the law forbidding trade with barbarians: what an absurd idea! Did the pirates who have visited our country repeatedly in the last hundred years arrive out of nowhere? If not, who invited them?

---

2. Source: Wan Ming, *Zhong Pu zao qi guan xi shi* (Beijing: She hui ke xue wen xian chu ban she, 2001), pp. 70–75.

43

Some say that in the Yuan dynasty, the ancient sage emperors cared only about their virtues and not exotic things. Now, envoys are often sent overseas with imperial edicts to summon the barbarians to trade. Considering the profits to be made on the trade in foreign commodities, how can these foreigners resist? During the reign of Yongle, the eunuch Zheng He was sent overseas—but even then some wondered if his voyages ran afoul of the founding emperor's prohibition on sea travel. Moreover, the lawless and the unregistered, ignoring the prohibition on private maritime voyages, opened ports for trade and invited the barbarians, thereby causing the catastrophes that have occurred in the past hundred years.

Tang Shunzhi

In terms of profit, ships are like mines. The best strategy is to close the mines and disperse the miners; if this cannot be done, the state should impose a monopoly, which is the second best strategy. If the mines are not closed or customs not imposed, all the profits are lost to the criminal gangs, which is no strategy at all. Nowadays, pirates occupy Nanao and other southern islands, openly profiting from trade with foreign ships. Chinese people supply and trade with these ships, and such trade is so profitable that not even the threat of the death penalty can deter them. It's been suggested that we should study the intentions behind the establishment of the maritime customs at the beginning of the dynasty in order to close gaps in profits and thwart the criminals. . . . Let us follow the fortifications of old, rely on the military of old, follow the land tax of old, and the maritime customs of old, and we can avoid all sorts of arguments.

Tang Shu

The pirates' frequent raids have devastated the localities and depleted the state treasury. . . . Given the differences between China and the barbarian nations, it's natural they should want to communicate with each other. China and the barbarian lands each have their own products, and it's hard to stop trade between the two since people will flock to wherever there is profit to be made. . . . After the sixth or seventh year of Jiajing (1527–28), the law [against private maritime trade] was enforced with greater severity. Once the commercial routes were blocked, the merchants lost their livelihood and turned to piracy. After the twentieth year of Jiajing (1541), when the ban on maritime travel was even more strictly enforced, the problem of piracy became even more serious. . . . Once the sea ban is lifted, those who are able can become merchants and the common people can be satisfied with their own livelihood.

Document 3

Gregory Martin, *Roma Sancta* (1581), excerpt describing the Jesuit College in Rome.[3]

The English priest Gregory Martin documented his experiences during his eighteen-month sojourn in Rome between the end of 1576 and July 1578. His enthusiastic encomium for the fathers of the Company echoed the fond memories of Ricci, years after the latter had left his alma mater.

Behold: in one house [Roman College], there is a whole university of learning and lessons.... The Audience is so full of Romans and Italians, Germans and Englishmen ... of others out of all the cities both young and old, of every faculty and profession.... What a goodly sight it is to see in the streets long trains of two and two, within the College a whole swarm, when hour after hour they come out of diverse schools into one court together, only to be succeeded by new companies taking other lessons with other readers. The School is full of desks to write upon, which there is so ordinary, that he is no earnest nor daily auditor that writes not every word, if the Reader dictate[s].... And as for the Readers, handpicked and carefully selected for their role, they are the very masters indeed of their faculties.

3. Source: Gregory Martin, *Roma Sancta (1581)*, edited by George Bruner Parks (Rome: Edizioni di Storia e Letteratura, 1969), pp. 162–63. I have modernized the spelling of Martin's text.

Document 4

Letter from the Jesuit missionary Nicolò Spinola, describing the dangers of sea voyage from Portugal to India, 1578.[4]

Embarking in a group of Jesuit missionaries from Lisbon to Goa, Spinola was traveling on a different ship from the one carrying Michele Ruggieri and Matteo Ricci. Relatively good sailing came to an abrupt halt at the Cape of Good Hope, where the ship ran into storms.

We had been sailing under a very good wind. But, after a few days, our Lord wanted to test us with a great storm that threatened danger and shipwreck; had our ship not been very strong we would have run the risk of getting lost on account of the headwind. We returned for five hundred miles back to the Cape of Good Hope with the passengers much afflicted, worrying that the currents would prevent us from leaving the said Cape. We experienced a strong contrary headwind for almost twenty-five days along with plenty of suffering, so that humanly speaking it was impossible to arrive this year at Goa, what with the great danger of hunger and thirst and other deprivations. Many were sick and few showed charity— love grows cold [Matthew 24:12]—because everyone was looking out for his own needs, having neither friend nor kin on-board. The crew received nothing but a bit of black biscuit and sour wine, and a small serving of olive oil once a month; they provided a glass and a half of water daily but soon considered giving less. All the poor wretches came to us for consolation, and we shared what little we had with them, paying particular attention to the sick as always. We hoped that our Lord would help us, that "the Lord's hand is not shortened" [Isaiah 59:1], and that he would show us great compassion.

---

4. Source: Letter of Nicolò Spinola to General Mercurian, Goa, October 26, 1578, in Joseph Wicki, editor, *Documenta Indica*, vol. XI (1577–80) (*Monumenta Historica Societatis Iesu*, vol. 103) (Rome: Institutum Historicum Societatis Iesu, 1970), pp. 314–15.

A storm rose. We all suffered terribly, as such great waves mixed with so much thunder and lighting in such a rough sea. This storm hit us near the land of Natale; it was not considered unusual, even though the sailors told me that they had never seen it on such a great scale. The lightning was so bright that people were blinded, and it seemed as if the ship were on fire. I have never seen or imagined such a thing; it seemed like hell was upon us. One had to be very close to Our Lord in order not to lose courage as we repeatedly faced death in this sudden and unexpectedly severe storm. Our resolve to face death, made before embarkation, did help us a lot, as we placed our lives in the hands of Our Lord.

Document 5

Ricci's letter to General Claudio Acquaviva, November 25, 1581, from Goa, India.[5]

After three years in India, Ricci had finished his theological studies and was ordained as a priest. He belonged to the small group of non-Portuguese Jesuits, mostly Italians, who were perhaps more critical of Portuguese ways, especially in the treatment of Indians. This letter written by Ricci to the General of the Society in Rome demonstrates an independence of mind and keen observation, qualities that would become even more prominent after his arrival in China.

This year the philosophy course began, and a change was made that some did not like. That is, none of the indigenous students—namely, the sons of the natives of India—could study philosophy and theology in our classes; they could only study Latin and casuistry, and thus it was carried out. And since this seems to me an important matter, I decided to record my opinions of it here. The superiors' reasons for enacting this change do not make sense to me: they say that, were the natives to learn their letters, they would become arrogant and not want to serve in lowly parishes; the superiors also say that the natives would thereafter pay little heed to those of us [European Jesuits] here who do not study or produce much in the way of fruitful work in philosophy and theology. But all of this could also be said (and perhaps with greater reason) about others who study at our schools here in India and in Europe. And yet, one does not avoid teaching everyone for this reason. Moreover, these indigenous people are seldom held in much esteem by other white people even if they, the natives, know a lot. Besides, it is the universal custom of the entire Society not to distinguish among persons; and particularly in India it was always the custom of many old, holy, and experienced fathers to open the schools to all, and welcome anyone who came.

---

5. Source: *Matteo Ricci, Lettere (1580–1609)*, edited by Francesco D'Arelli (Macerata: Quodlibet, 2001), p. 31.

Secondly, if we make this change we are going to foster ignorance among the ministers of the Church in a place where knowledge is so necessary. [The indigenous people we are training] to be priests will be charged with the care of souls, and it does not seem expedient that, among so many kinds of infidels, priests should be so ignorant that they can neither respond to an argument nor offer to confirm themselves or others in our faith (even if we do not want to hope for miracles when unnecessary); a priest trained only in casuistry will not be able to accomplish all this. And the third reason, the one that moves me the most, is that these people are very much debased in our land, and nobody will help them except for us [Jesuits]; for this reason they have shown us much love. Should they discover that the same fathers are now against them and do not wish them to hold their heads high and obtain the sorts of benefices or posts among the members [of the Society] one could otherwise obtain by studying, I doubt very much they would not come to hate us, and this would obstruct the main purpose of the Company in India—that is, the conversion of nonbelievers and maintaining them in our holy faith.

Document 6

Ricci's letters from Macao to Martino de Fornari and Claudio Acquaviva, February 13, 1583.[6]

One of the first letters written by Ricci from China, it shows his early and keen interest in the power structure of Ming China and his affinity for the mandarins.

China is grand in many ways; it certainly has the greatest king in the world. This king's grandeur is shown by the fact that he rules over such a large and fertile part of the world. He does not have lords in his land, but rather governors he appoints at his pleasure. These governors enjoy such esteem among those they rule that they are like gods on earth, and are treated as such in both private and public. At home they do not speak with anyone from the outside. In public, they speak only in a suitably large, church-like hall or corridor, where the *lao tia* [i.e. laodie 老爹, literally "venerable lord," an honorific for mandarins] as they call him, is seated in a chair at the end, just as in a chapel, behind a table carrying a decorated front, just like an altar. He wears a very unusual vestment and a hat to which is attached ears, much larger than horses' ears, made of cloth; like the red hats of cardinals, these hats are signs of the lords' dignity. In the middle of [the hall] is a wide, well-made path that leads to doors through which only the governor can come and go. On the sides of this room are two other doors where the others enter, and many armed men stand guard, according to rank, either close to the governor or outside the door. And when one speaks to the governor it has to be on one's knees, more than a stone's throw away, and in a loud voice; and once the lord has received one's message or has given an answer, one must leave in a rush, for the lord can give such cruel beatings, on account of small things, that many die; he can dole out such beatings as casually as one of our teachers might to a student.

---

6. Source: *Matteo Ricci, Lettere (1580–1609)*, edited by Francesco D'Arelli (Macerata: Quodlibet, 2001), pp. 46–47.

Document 7

Ricci's letter to Juan Bautista Roman, September 13, 1584, describing statecraft and religion in China (excerpts).[7]

Ricci's early assessment of Chinese civilization represents a mix of positive and negative views. Confident in the scientific and religious superiority of the West, Ricci was nonetheless genuinely impressed by Chinese philosophy, astronomy, engineering, and especially statecraft. Perceptively he noted the low social status of all things military in Ming China and associated it unfavorably with the unmanly culture of the literati, comparing it with the sense of honor and violence in Europe.

The knowledge of the Chinese can be seen in the invention of their characters, so graceful yet difficult, having one character for each thing, written in a most complicated and complex way . . . nonetheless they all study and learn these, and through them they acquire their disciplines, in which they are very learned, in medicine, in moral physics, in mathematics and in astrology. It is admirable that they can calculate very clearly and precisely the eclipses, in a manner different from ours, and how this people, who have never had any commerce with Europe, have achieved in arithmetic and in all the liberal and mechanical arts by themselves as much as we have, who had obtained this knowledge through our communication with the whole world. I only wish that Your Grace judge the Chinese through their statecraft, into which they have put all their effort and achieved such brilliance that they leave all other nations behind. If to their natural ingenuity God is to add the divine understanding of our holy Catholic faith, it would seem to me that Plato could imagine no better republic than what exists in reality in China. . . .

China is governed by a single monarch, who succeeds by primogeniture. The present ruler Vanlie [Wanli], twenty-four years old, has

---

7. Source: *Matteo Ricci, Lettere (1580–1609)*, edited by Francesco D'Arelli (Macerata: Quodlibet, 2001), pp. 57–87.

governed for twelve years. . . . The ruler governs his whole realm through magistrates, called mandarins, and they are of two categories: The first, who obtain through their own bravery and by succeeding those who first conquered the reign, are officers of war. . . . The other category are the mandarins of letters who are much more important and superior to those of war. All are divided into nine grades, and each grade has so many kinds of office that it will take a lot of time for us to understand. . . .

The power and state of China is founded more on the large population, numerous cities, and good governance rather than on walls, fortifications, and the indigenous ability for war. . . . The Chinese are little trained in war and in military arts, and they hold [soldiers] in low esteem. The military is considered one of the four lowest classes in the republic because . . . the majority of the soldiers are malefactors from the lower classes condemned to perpetual servitude by the monarch. Only the pirates force them to bestir themselves, since they sail on two or three ships from Japan landing on the Chinese coast, seizing towns big and small in the land, putting everything to the torch and the sword without any resistance. . . . They say the Tartars also stir them to action along the borders, but to tell the truth, whatever they write to Your Majesty about the Chinese, it cannot be said they are warriors, since both in the way they look and in their hearts they are more like women. If anyone shows them his teeth, they immediately humiliate themselves—yet they immediately put their foot on the neck of those who subject themselves to them. Every morning they spend two hours combing their hair and dressing, taking all the time in the world. Fleeing is not a dishonor to them, and they know neither injuries nor insults, as it is with us, having only a feminine anger. . . .

Document 8

A Chinese poem by Michele Ruggieri and an excerpt on his missionary strategy.

Ruggieri was Ricci's first companion in China and the first Jesuit to learn Chinese. The first text is a poem composed by Ruggieri in the mid-1580s showing both a good command of classical Chinese as well as interest in Buddhism; the second is an excerpt from Ruggieri's manuscript journal, written after he had left China in 1588 to return to Italy, that contains his recommendation for future evangelization strategies in China. Note the contrast between Ruggieri's sympathies for Buddhism and Ricci's strong antagonism (see Documents 17 and 23).

A poem written while in residence at the Tianchu ci for Some Gentlemen:

> On a small barge I set sail from the seashore,
> And came to China after a three years' voyage;
> Like autumn water my mind is always clear and bright;
> The Body is like a bodhi so how can there be flowers?[8]
> If you do me the honor to allow me to stay,
> Forthwith shall I take up my abode.
> And if you ask me about the things of the Western paradise,
> My explanation is not that of Buddha Sakya.[9]

---

8. This is an allusion to the famous answer by the Sixth Patriarch Huineng to the question of his master of the way to keep pure: "Bodhi originally has no tree, so how can it be dirty?" Ruggieri's Chinese poem strives for the effect of Chan meditation, which is missed in Father Chan's English translation.

9. Source: Albert Chan, S.J., "Michele Ruggieri, S.J. (1543–1607) and His Chinese Poems," *Monumenta Serica* 41 (1993), pp. 129–76, here, pp. 158–59. I have modified the translation by Chan. The Chinese verses read: 一葉扁舟泛海涯, 三年水路到中華, 心如秋水常涵月, 身若菩提那有花, 貴省肯容吾著步, 貧僧至此便為家, 諸君若問西天事, 非是如來佛釋迦.

If our fathers could sustain themselves with herbs, fruits, vegetables, rice and grain, and abstain from eating meat, fish, dairy products, and living things, they would acquire great credit in China and would make many conversions. This diet was supposedly established by their sect of idolaters (i.e. Buddhist clerics), who prohibited the killing of animals in accordance with the teachings of Pythagoras. But since all of this is held in great veneration by the powerful people of China, from the emperor and the people, who still respect this false doctrine; and since [the idolaters] are summoned by the emperor and the powerful, as one can read in their histories, and given donations of large sums of money, for building temples and other pious works, we would achieve all the more because our doctrines are more true and holy than theirs. In their [Buddhist] doctrines, I have read a chapter that speaks about this and argues for this abstinence as an effective means for the chastity and purity that are suitable to priests and not to the superstitions of that sect.[10]

---

10. Source: Archivum Romanum Societatis Iesu, Jap-Sin 101, fol. 109^v.

Document 9

Account of Ruggieri's encounter with Buddhist monks during his travels in the winter of 1585–86 to Zhejiang.[11]

In November 1585, Ruggieri met with a brother of Wang Pan, the Jesuits' mandarin patron in Zhaoqing. This brother had traveled from their hometown Shaoxing in Zhejiang province to Guang-zhou in order to trade with the Portuguese in Macao. Ruggieri acted as the middleman and took this opportunity to get a new missionary, the young Portuguese Jesuit Antonio de Almeida to join him. Together, the party set out from Guangzhou in early November to return to Shaoxing, where Ruggieri hoped to estab-lish a new missionary base. After sailing by boat through Guang-dong and Jiangxi, they arrived at the border between Jiangxi and Zhejiang and exchanged river transport for land. They stayed for three days at Gaolin.

A lot of people came to see them.... They were invited by a protector of the idols to a festival in his temple, and the Jesuit fathers deemed it expedient to attend—not in order to pay attention to the idols, but in order to criti-cize them for worshiping false gods. There were many altars with cloth coverings, and many Buddhist monks dressed in caps and silk dalmatics recited prayers and performed their ceremonies. The Buddhist monks received Ruggieri's party with great love, ate with them at a banquet, and showed the fathers particular love and reverence. Ruggieri and Almeida gave the monks some copies of the catechism in their language, in which

---

11. Source: Archivum Romanum Societatis Iesu, Jap-Sin 101 I, fol. 44. This representa-tion of Guanyin seems to have combined the iconographic motifs of the "Water-Moon Guanyin" ("Water-Moon" is the name of the posture and does not involve a representa-tion of the moon), and the "Son-Giving Guanyin," often depicted as riding on a wondrous beast. Ruggieri's explanation to Almeida refers to the legend of Princess Miaoshan, who would become the "Thousand-Eye and Thousand-Arm Guanyin." Princess Miaoshan, however, was the third daughter of King Miao Zhuang, not the "only" daughter. This is puzzling.

the falsity of the idol is confuted in one chapter; and it seemed to all of them that this was a most excellent doctrine. Here our fathers saw how the devil counterfeited the ceremonies of the holy Catholic Church and mimicked them so effectively that Father Antonio de Almeida, the companion of Father Ruggieri, would easily have been deceived into thinking that the painted lady holding the dragon and the moon under her feet could have been the image of the Queen of Heaven—since all around in the temple were hung many paintings of miracles, with [ex voto in the shape of] eyes and feet made of wax, silver, and gold, such as one would see in the famous churches dedicated to Our Lady in our Europe—had not Father Ruggieri told him that she was the only daughter of the King of China by the name of Cunn-in.

Document 10

Excerpts from relevant passages of *Della entrata* on the missionary work of the Jesuits in Zhaoqing, their relationship with their mandarin patrons, and Ricci's scientific work.[12]

Ruggieri and Ricci arrived in Zhaoqing, Guangdong province, in September 1583. The missionaries depended on the patronage of the mandarins, of whom the district magistrate Wang Pan was their chief protector. A devout Buddhist, Wang Pan thought of the Europeans as Indian monks since Ruggieri introduced himself as such, and asked the Jesuits to shave their hair and beards and dress in the style of Chinese Buddhist monks.

[p. 180] [September 1583] In Zhaoqing they were immediately taken to the palace of the Prefect [*zhifu*] Wang Pan, who was giving audience, and from whom we were received with much benevolence; nonetheless we were kneeling like all the others who spoke to him in audience. He asked who we were, where we came from, and what we wanted. Through an interpreter, they replied, "we are religious men who serve God, the Lord of Heaven, and come from the Extreme West, having traveled three or four years, on account of the reputation of the good governance of China. We wish only to remain here, where, free from the noise of commerce and other secular things in Macao, we could build a small house and chapel and spend the rest of our lives serving God."

* * *

[pp. 185–86] Close to the temple of Tiennin [Tianningci 天寧, Buddhist temple where Ruggieri and Ricci lived], where the fathers stayed the first time [Ruggieri and Francisco Pasio in 1582], there lived a youth of great intelligence by the name of Nico Chen. Being a neighbor he was in

---

12. Source: *Fonti Ricciane*, edited by Pasquale D'Elia (Rome: La Libreria dello Stato, 1942–49), vol. 1, book 2, chapters 3, 4, and 5, pp. 180, 185–86, 197, 199, 207, 209–10.

contact with the fathers all the months of their first stay, and became a good friend, and they thought to make him a Christian. They taught him many things of the holy Catholic faith and drew him to it; for that reason, at their departure, they left with him the altar on which they said mass, as if he were already almost Christian. The next time Ruggieri and Ricci visited Chen, they found that he had placed the altar in a cubicle in his house; and since he did not have any other images, he wrote on a tablet in the middle of the wall two large Chinese characters that meant "To the Lord of Heaven" [i.e. Tianzhu]. On the altar were seven or eight lamps, and here he lit his incense, adored and prayed to the God of which he had already some knowledge.

* * *

[p. 197] Since many literati wanted to know more than the Ten Commandments which we had printed, the fathers, together with a scholar in the residence, composed a catechism in their language [*Tianzhu shilu* by Ruggieri], in which they refuted some points of the sects of China and explained the main doctrines of the holy faith . . . ; and all the important people, especially the Prefect Wang Pan, received printed copies with great joy.

* * *

[p. 199] When important magistrates wish to grant a great favor to some person, they send, with great solemnity and general jubilation, a framed wooden frontispiece on which they write and carve three or four very large and meaningful characters in praise of that person. . . . And so the magistrate of the city [Wang Pan] and protector of the fathers did this favor . . . sending them two such frontispieces, one for placing on top of the house door, which was the same as the chapel, saying, in Chinese, "Church of the flower of saints"; the other was for placing in the hall, which said, "People coming from the holy land of the West."[13]

* * *

---

13. In *Della entrata* (FR, vol. 1, p. 199), Ricci ignored the Buddhist significance of the characters and inaccurately translated the four Chinese characters, which means only "Pure Land of the West," into "people coming from the holy land of the West." The first expression was interpreted by Ruggieri as a reference to the Virgin Mary, flower of the Saints.

[p. 207] The fathers had in their hall a map of the world in our language . . . all the important people wanted to have this map translated into Chinese in order to better know its contents. For this reason the Prefect ordered Father Matteo, who already knew some Chinese, to translate all the annotations of the map since he wanted to print and circulate it in all of China. . . . The father, who had a sufficient knowledge of mathematics (since he was for some years the disciple of Father Cristoforo Clavio [Christoph Klau] in Rome), undertook this work with the help of a [Chinese] literary friend. In a short time a world map bigger than the one in the house, with other annotations and explanations adapted to China, was made.

* * *

[pp. 209–10] When [the Chinese] saw that the world was so large, with China confined to one corner of [the map] (and so small in their opinion), the ignorant ones began to ridicule and scorn. But those more learned, seeing the beautiful order of the lines of latitude and longitude, of the equinoxes, the tropics, and the five zones, with the customs of the different countries and the whole world full of different names translated from the first map now printed, which gave credit to this novelty, could not but believe that all of this was truth.

Document 11

Alessandro Valignano and Alonso Sanchez: Two Jesuit views on evangelization in East Asia, 1581–88.

The texts below vividly illustrate diametrically opposite views of evangelization in East Asia within the Society of Jesus. The first texts were written by Alessandro Valignano (1539–1606), an Italian Jesuit appointed in 1573 as Visitor to the Asian missions. Acting on behalf of the General in Rome, Valignano was the most powerful Jesuit in Portuguese Asia in determining missionary tactics and strategies. The founder of the policy of "cultural accommodation," Valignano, based on his Japanese experience, summoned Ruggieri from India to Macao to study Chinese and later approved Ricci's strategy to win over the Chinese Confucian scholars. The first three excerpts come from Valignano's missionary directives in Japan; and the fourth text comes from a letter in which Valignano excoriates the views of a fellow Jesuit, the Spaniard Alonso Sanchez.

One of the first Jesuits to visit the Philippines, the newest realm of Habsburg Spain, Alonso Sanchez (1547–93) was co-opted by the Spanish governor to carry out diplomatic missions to China in 1582. In 1587–88, Sanchez returned to Spain via Mexico, bringing with him the first report of the government in Manila to which he added a long memorandum on the "entry" or conquest of China. Severely criticized by his fellow Spanish Jesuit José de Acosta and by Valignano, Sanchez nevertheless obtained a hearing from King Philip II, but the defeat of the Spanish Armada in 1588 by the English dashed this fantastical plan to conquer China. Despite criticisms, Sanchez ended his career as Provincial of the Jesuits in Spain.

Alessandro Valignano on Conversion in Japan[14]

Let us be mature and prudent in places where new conversions start. Even if the local lord and many of his vassals become Christians, avoid drawing attention by destroying his temples and engaging in similar repugnant acts. Even when a convert desires to do so, they should not be allowed to do so. The idols should be gathered and burned in secrecy little by little. The temples should be transformed into churches or put to other convenient use, so that they remain, thereby preventing the gentiles from saying that wherever we enter, we bring destruction and desolation to everything.

* * *

To consult the Japanese brothers or our prudent friends on every matter is also very important in order to keep up a good reputation among the people. This is because Japanese customs and courtesies are so different from those of the Southern Barbarians [i.e. Portuguese] that, without their advice, we will not be able to make the right decisions.

* * *

When preaching the Gospel, we should avoid mixing in European customs not needed for the salvation of souls. Those of our customs that run contrary to Japanese customs will not only be rejected but will also cause the rejection of the Gospel itself; for example, marriages with special conditions, the division of inheritance according to our rules, and things of this kind. Unless they are clearly against divine law, we should follow the Japanese ways in all these things.

---

14. Source: Valignano, *Il Cerimoniale per i missionarii del Giappone* (1581) and *Sumario de las cosas de Japón* (1583), cited in Renzo de Luca, "The Politics of Evangelization: Valignano and His Relations with the Japanese Rulers of the Sixteenth Century," in *Alessandro Valignano, S.I.: Uomo del Rinascimento: Ponte tra Oriente e Occidente*, edited by Adolfo Tamburello, A. Antoni Ücerler, and Marisa Di Russo (Rome: Institutum Historicum Societatis Iesu, 2008), pp. 145–56.

Valignano on Sanchez[15]

… And even if I do not pass judgment on his spirit, nonetheless, I say to Your Paternity that it seems to me this spirit is very dangerous and deviates from the *Institutes* of the Society, and is based on personal, subjective values and indiscretion.

Alonso Sanchez: Memorandum to Philip II on the Conquest of China[16]

On the Rights and Title of Entry

First, concerning the right and justification for entering and pacifying this reign, the father who goes to Spain [Sanchez] has discussed this matter many times in those parts ruled by the Castilians [i.e. the Philippines], as well as in the parts ruled by the Portuguese of India, China, and Japan with all learned persons and those of good conscience and experience, and knows what all feel in this case—that is, that he should deal with and confer with Your Majesty, and as it pleases him insofar as necessary, confer about what he has heard, knows, and deems appropriate on the rights and titles which apply here, by invoking the preaching of the Gospels as well as the grievances that those on these islands [the Philippines], and especially the Portuguese in Macao, face every day [toward the Chinese], which are the two sources and roots for rights and titles justifying this entry.

On the Necessary Means for This Entry, Firstly of People

First, considering the location and land of China and her people, it will be sufficient that ten to twelve thousand men come [to China] from Spain, Italy, and Your Majesty's other realms, and it should be desirable that as many of these men as possible be Biscayans [seafarers from the Basque province of Vizcaya in Spain], and that the armada be dispatched from

---

15. Source: Letter of Valignano to Acquaviva, Goa, April 1, 1585, *Documenta Indica*, vol. XIV, edited by Joseph Wicki, p. 11.

16. Source: Francisco Colin, *Labor evangelica: Ministerios Apostolicos de los Obreros de la Compañia de Iesus, fundacion, y progressos de su Provincia en las Islas Filipinas,* edited by Pablo Pastells, 3 vols. (Barcelona: Henrich, 1900–1902), vol. 1, pp. 438, 441–42.

Vizcaya. To those men can be added some five to six thousand Japanese and as many Visayans [from the southern provinces of the Philippines], vassals of Your Majesty in our Islands, who are high-spirited and strong.

* * *

When the time comes—and before the Chinese hear of the news of the armada—the fathers of the Company [i.e. Ruggieri and Ricci] who are inside China in the city of Jaoquin [Zhaoqing] should be sought out in order that they can supply intelligence to the armada about the land, their strength, troops, equipment, and whatever dangers and advice, as well as serve as interpreters in order to persuade the Chinese to accept the entry peacefully, to hear and receive the preachers and law that God has sent to them, and the help that His Majesty wants to provide in order that they may receive the faith without fear, and how he gives them such a great benefit of liberation from the tyranny of their mandarins and from the yoke and servitude they now endure, granting them the liberty of both body and soul....

* * *

On the Fruits of This Conquest

... [T]he second is that nobody, except for those who have seen them, can grasp the great quantity of innumerable souls, who will come to know and adore their creator, who are now in a state of blindness, ignorance, and servitude to the devil....

The third is ... aside from the corruption of sin and the depravity of the evil and old habits, this people is naturally so good, noble, delightful, suave, and easy to govern ... and all of China ... is in such peace and quiet that nowhere else has been known and discovered in the New and Old worlds [such a condition] without any aid deriving from supernatural light, fear, or reward, but only through the force, or better said, the suavity of a good natural government.

Document 12

Excerpts from letters written by Ricci to General Claudio Acquaviva, Shaozhou, November 15, 1592, and January 15 and 17, 1593.[17]

The years in Shaozhou were a difficult time for Ricci: two of his close companions died; he received news of his grandmother's death from Italy; and armed robbers broke into the Jesuit residence, an incident in which Ricci badly injured his foot. Nonetheless, he made important progress in evangelization and in studying Confucian texts. Most of the converts were devout Buddhists, although Ricci's new turn to Confucianism would prefigure his later missionary strategy and his future success.

This year I made a trip with one of our brothers [Chinese Jesuit brothers from Macao] to a famous city, four or five days away, called Nanhiom [Nanxiong]. . . . There was a Christian by the name of Giuseppe in this city, who was baptized last year [1591] in our residence, having come by himself to learn the things of his salvation. . . . Our Christian is a merchant who employs thirty to forty people in his commerce. . . . This Christian is held in much esteem and considered holy in these parts for having a good conscience, before becoming a Christian and, in spite of his age, for fasting at all times according to the local fashion, that is never eating meat or fish or eggs or similar food, but sustaining himself on vegetables and similar food.

* * *

I noticed that most of these people whom I visited came from other provinces, and it is true what they say that in other provinces of China [other than Guangdong] there are many more people who believe in the immortality of the soul and care about their salvation. . . . In these few

---

17. Source: *Matteo Ricci, Lettere (1580–1609)*, edited by Francesco D'Arelli (Macerata: Quodlibet, 2001), pp. 169–80.

days spent in this house [Giuseppe's] we selected some who were most apt to receive holy baptism and baptized ten adults and children much to our consolation and that of Giuseppe, who said with tears of joy in his eyes that we have come so far to sanctify his house, and among those baptized were his son, a brother, and other relatives. This number would have been much greater if this Christian did not have a false opinion, namely, that to become Christian meant leaving the world and becoming a hermit, having nothing to do with the things of this life, just as he had done, leaving his wife and all household affairs, paying attention only to his salvation, intervening little in business; also, being a Gentile, he was much given to meditating in the manner of the Gentile sects [i.e. Buddhist Chan meditation], which is not too different from ours, always entreating me to teach him our meditations since he is already old and does not have much time to do more good for his soul. . . .

* * *

The whole year we were busy in studies and I finished teaching to my companion father a course on moral philosophy in Chinese literary texts, which are the *Four Books*, good moral texts by four good philosophers. This year the father Visitor [Alessandro Valignano] ordered me to translate these into Latin in order to help me prepare a new catechism in their language, of which we have a great need, since the other, which was composed in the beginning [Ruggieri's *Tianzhu shilu*], has not succeeded as well as it should.

Document 13

Excerpt from a description of Ricci by a mandarin in Shaozhou, written ca. 1592.[18]

This biography of Ricci was written by Liu Chengfan, who was vice-prefect in the Prefecture of Shaozhou (韶州府同知) during Ricci's years in Guangdong province. It provides an exceptionally vivid picture of the Jesuit in the persona of a western (Buddhist) monk. A highly valuable document, this narrative offers information unavailable in other historical sources and presents a picture of the westerner different from Ricci's self-representation in his later memoirs. Three themes stand out: first, the fortune of the Jesuits was tied to the continued unease of the Chinese with Portuguese Macao, and there is a clear policy debate among Guangdong officials on this matter; second, we have to remember that Ricci was dressed as a Buddhist monk at this time, and his words and behavior seemed consistent with this adopted persona despite his repudiation of this early experience in the memoirs; third, even in these early years, Ricci excelled in Confucian learning and made a tremendous impression on his mandarin interlocutors. All the important data on Ricci are included in this excerpt. The text was first published in Liu Houqing, compiler, Liu shi zupu (Genealogy of the Liu clan), 1914. It was rediscovered in 2010.

Li Madou[19] was an eminent monk from the Western Region, with the sobriquet of Xitai.[20] Traveling with his brother monk Tianyou Chongjiu[21] to Duanzhou [Zhaoqing[22]] in Guangdong, they stayed in

---

18. Source: Liu Mingqiang, *Wanli Shaozhou tong zhi Liu Chengfan yi qi tong zhi* in *Shaoguan xueyuan xuebao* 11 (2010), pp. 1–8.

19. Ricci's Chinese name.

20. Meaning "the most eminent of the West."

21. This must have been Michele Ruggieri. This is the only source where Ruggieri's Buddhist name is recorded.

22. Duanzhou was the Song dynasty name for Zhaoqing, when it was first established as a district.

an ancient monastery, purchased stones and bricks to construct a tall pagoda.[23] . . . [In 1589] Sir Chen Hailou of eastern Zhejiang and I were stationed in Shaozhou and visited Duanzhou on official business to see Supreme Commander (*zongdu*) Liu,[24] lodging for the night in our boat by the pagoda.[25] . . . In the morning, Monk Li embarked to offer us tea. We discovered he was a European. He has a protruding forehead and deeply set eyes, with light-colored hair and dark beard, exerting an exotic presence. The tea he served was fragrant and gave me a fresh lift under the arms. When he saw my poem at the desk, he asked for it. So I asked the clerk to make a copy for him.

After two months, I visited Duanzhou again on pressing matters, for the Supreme Commander (*zongdu*) had invited me to discuss military affairs. He told me in confidence: "According to the report of the officials in Weizhou and Chaozhou, the pirate Chen has been in collusion with the Ryukyuans, killing and robbing and posing a major threat to our security. Also, Macao used to be the site where the various barbarian tribute-bearing ships would arrive.[26] Now, the law has become lax, and I have heard that barbarians who do not acknowledge our legitimate rule pretend to bear tribute and have been trading there. This is a potential threat that cannot be ignored for long. My office wishes to demonstrate the authority of the celestial kingdom and annihilate these pirates with our navy. Then I learned that there are two monks from Europe in the southern seas who are staying here illegally.[27] There is a danger that military secrets may be leaked. You will transmit my orders and decree to them: "In Shaozhou there is the Nanhua monastery, where the Sixth

---

23. Construction of the Chongxi Pagoda began at about the same time that Ruggieri and Ricci arrived in Zhaoqing. Although it was not built by the Jesuits, the Jesuit residence was adjacent to the pagoda, hence the association in the minds of many between the Jesuits and the pagoda.

24. This was Liu Jiezhai, appointed *zongdu* of Guangxi and Guangdong in 1589.

25. Zhaoqing lies on the bank of the Xijiang (West River) and was accessible by boat from Shaozhou.

26. In the 15th century tribute-bearing ships would arrive in Guangzhou, not Macao, but embassies from Southeast Asia had stopped by the early 16th century.

27. Ricci and the young Portuguese Jesuit Antonio de Almeida.

Patriarch[28] had taught and where the waters of the Cao Brook taste as sweet as that in the Western Paradise. Should you not move there? . . . As to the cost of building the pagoda my office will reimburse you double." I nodded my agreement and left. The same day I summoned the monk, but before I could open my mouth, he said: "What you, Sir, are about to decree: Is it not that the Supreme Commander wishes to search Macao? This matter does not hinder my work, and how would I dare to leak any news?" I said: "How do you know this? Did any officers of the Supreme Commander pass this onto you?" He answered: "Your monk, my humble self, has crossed oceans and many capitals, traveling tens of thousands of miles, how can I not predict people's intentions? I would be willing to move to Nanhua monastery." When the conversation came to compensation for the pagoda, he said: "What the Supreme Commander hopes from his military expedition is surely advancement in his career. I, a monk, look upon the Chinese and all barbarians as one; even this illusory body is empty. What need do I have for money? But human lives are precious and military actions exact their cost. If you, Sir, simply follow his will and execute this, I am afraid the ghosts and spirits will ask for an accounting." When I heard his words I was very frightened. The next morning I visited the Supreme Commander and asked him discreetly: "Sir, have you consulted your commanders about the proposed campaign?" Liu answered: "This is an important matter; I have not even consulted the district magistrates and intendants. I have confided in you because I know of your discretion." The same day, the two monks also visited the Supreme Commander to take leave. In preparing their luggage they took nothing from the pagoda except for several cases of books. Just as they were loading these onto the boat, the Supreme Commander dispatched someone to examine them. All they were carrying were volumes from the *Six Classics*, *The Analects*, *Mencius*, *Xin jian* (Examination of Nature), and *Shiji* (History by Sima Qian). Pleased with this, the Supreme Commander sent some gifts, but the two monks declined them and left for Nanhua.

[*The following section narrates the visit to Xiangshan county by the author on the pretext of examining military finances; in reality he was actually investigating the Portuguese in Macao. The district magistrate Xu accompanied*

---

28. Huineng (638–713), a native of Guangdong, was the founder of the southern school of Chan meditation and the Sixth Patriarch in the line of transmission according to Chan tradition.

Liu to Macao. When they questioned the foreigners, they all answered they were lured to Macao by Chinese collaborators. Magistrate Xu spoke against a military expedition against Macao. Military wages in Guangdong depended on customs taxes. Any military action would frighten off the foreigners, and there would be no money to pay the troops. Liu then composed a memorial arguing that the Portuguese in Macao did not present a threat. Previously, ships from Champa, Siam, and Vietnam had sailed there to trade. If a military expedition had been sent, all the rich barbarians would have long fled with their wealth. Frustrated with their futile operation, the soldiers would simply kill civilians to claim victory. No good would result from a campaign of suppression, whereas toleration would bring trade and prosperity and encourage the barbarians to become civilized. Supreme Commander Liu endorsed the memorandum and the plan to suppress Portuguese Macao was shelved.]

After a month, the monk Li came to Shaozhou to visit me and the magistrate Chen. He said: "I dared not disobey Supreme Commander Liu's command to move to Nanhua monastery, but the monks there eat meat and drink wine, completely ignoring the rules of the Sixth Patriarch. I am ashamed to be with them. Moreover, it is far from the district seat and rumors can easily arise. May I move to Guangxiao Monastery outside the city to observe their monastic practice?" . . . The monastery is to the west of the district seat across the river at Fuyun Hill, where the Sixth Patriarch wrote his sutra. Monk Li acquired a piece of land next to it for his residence.

On the ninth of the ninth month an octagonal pavilion was built . . . the pavilion consisted of three floors. The top is dedicated to the Mother of the Lord of Heaven and the middle to the Lord of Heaven; there are no other shrines. There are also several rooms to house books, all works from the orthodox Confucian Canon, from history and philosophy.[29] When asked about his own translated work, [he replied] there is only *Dayin quantu* (Map of the World).[30]

Sir Chen and I interrogated [Ricci]: "According to Chinese traditions, Damo (Bodhidharma, a 5th- to 6th-century CE monk) came from the West, and is called Amitabuddha. Therefore, all who follow Buddhist dharma respect the Three Jewels.[31] In the Tang dynasty, the sutras also

---

29. This is the only description of the Jesuit residence in Shaozhou.

30. See Document 24.

31. Buddha, *dharma* (learning), and *sangha* (the Buddhist community of clerics) constitute the three most precious aspects in all Buddhist traditions.

came from the West. Since then, there have been many branches and sects, and those professing to be Buddhists and studying sutras are numerous. You are a western monk, yet you reject this. Is it because you have studied *Mozi*[32] and refuse to follow their teachings?" He answered: "There are no fewer than two hundred city states in the West. This Amitabuddha mentioned earlier could be a sect leader of another country. There is no such person in my Europe. What is the most exalted in the world if not the heaven ruled by the lord god? And this god is born of this mother, and so my country only worships one god. . . ."

We then asked about his books and he answered: "I have come to visit your esteemed country only on account of a few books. I first translated them in Vietnam and then visited dozens of other lands, and nothing appealed to my heart. I then retranslated it and visited Siam, and then dozens of other lands, and nothing appealed to my heart. I then translated it the third time in Champa, the fourth time in the Ryukyu, the fifth time on the island of Formosa.[33] I have visited more than one hundred lands in ten years and yet I did not see a single person carrying a book.[34] When I asked for the way, everyone praised Guangzhou, and so I translated the work into Chinese and entered Guangdong. When I saw the books in the markets, I was very pleased and regretted only I did not recognize Chinese characters. Therefore, I looked for a good master. The next day, a scholar arrived and said: "I have heard that you monk wish to find a good teacher, is that right?" I said: "I need one teacher for the *Six Classics* and another for the *Four Books* and various histories."[35] The

---

32. Book written by this philosopher who lived in the late 5th century BCE; Mozi taught pacifism, universal love, and austerity, and mocked the followers of Confucius for their social distinctions and obsession with rituals.

33. The Chinese term is Fudao, the island of Fu. Could Ricci be referring to Formosa, the Portuguese term for Taiwan?

34. Clearly, Ricci is not beyond exaggeration and invention in making his point.

35. Canonical learning in the Ming dynasty consisted of studies of the *Four Books* and *Five Classics*. The *Four Books* refer to *The Analects* (collection of sayings by Confucius by his disciples), *Daxue* (Great Learning), *Zhongyong* (Doctrine of the Mean), and *Mencius* (collection of discourses by Mencius). These books were compiled at the time of Confucius and the successive generations of his disciples. The *Five Classics* represented more ancient texts that were edited by Confucius as essential learning for the gentleman; they consist of *Yijing* (Book of Changes), a book of divination, *Shujing* (Book of Documents), containing recorded speeches and historical events from ancient history, *Shijing* (Book of Poetry), *Liji* (Records of Rites), and the *Chunqiu Zuozhuan* (Spring and Autumn Annals

scholar replied: "There are only *Five Classics*, not *Six Classics*. You have been misled." I said: "The poetry of your compatriot Chen Baisha[36] has spread to my country and the verse 'the virtue of the *Six Classics* fills the waterways.' Is this also mistaken?" He left without a word. . . .

Not long thereafter, the magistrate of Nanxiong, Sir Sun of Weinan, came to Shaozhou on official business. He asked me: "Is there a western monk in your jurisdiction?" I said: "Indeed." "Is he well versed in the classics and history?" I replied: "He has books, but I do not know whether he is well versed in them." So, Sun and I visited him. Sun specialized in the *Book of Poetry* (*Shijing*) and asked him about the poems *Jingmin* and *Yuanliao*. I specialized in the *Book of Changes* (*Yijing*) and asked him about the passage on 'Heaven and Earth.' The monk knew all the texts. Sun smiled at me and said: "We each study one classic and the monk knows both; have we not made ourselves ridiculous in his eyes?"[37] We took leave and after that the monk's reputation spread. When officials visited Shaozhou, there were some who did not enter the city and only visited the western monk.

---

and Commentary of Zuo), a chronicle with commentary on events of the Spring and Autumn period. The *Sixth Classic* that Ricci referred to is a lost text on music.

36. Chen Baisha (1428–1500) was one of the most famous scholars and poets during the Ming dynasty. He was born in Xinhui in Guangdong province.

37. The imperial civil service examination during the Ming dynasty required candidates to write obligatory examination papers on the *Four Books*, but they could choose one of the *Five Classics* as their specialty. The *Shujing* and the *Yijing* were the most popular texts with examination candidates, because it was easier (and more pleasurable) to memorize poetry, and the *Yijing* is the shortest of the *Five Classics*.

Document 14

The first impression of Ricci by Qu Rukui (written in 1599 and recalling events from the 1580s).[38]

A prodigal son from an elevated family in Changshu in the Jiang-nan region (his father was the Minister of Rites in Nanjing), Qu was Ricci's first important Chinese convert. Attracted by Ricci's charisma, Qu was initially interested in learning alchemy from Ricci before focusing his interest in mathematics. A close friend of the Jesuit, Qu advised Ricci to abandon his Buddhist persona and assume that of the Confucian scholar. Baptized only toward the end of Ricci's life, Qu named his son Matteo after his friend.

In the yinchou year of Wanli [1589], I, the ineloquent, was visiting Mount Luo fu 羅浮 [near Guangzhou]; on the occasion of visiting Viceroy Sir Liu Jiezhai, I met the Venerable Li [Ricci's Chinese name was Li Madou] in Zhaoqing. The moment I saw him, I was struck by his look of distinction. And when Sir Viceroy moved Li to Shaozhou, I happened to be passing through Nanhua Monastery and again encountered him. Thus, I studied numerical correspondences between the heavens and earth [i.e. mathematics and astronomy] with him for two years before departing.

---

38. Source: Qu Rukui's preface to Ricci's *On Friendship*, in *Li Madou zhong wen zhu yi ji*, edited by Zhu Weizheng (Shanghai: Fu dan da xue chu ban she, 2001), p. 117.

Document 15

Excerpts from a letter by Ricci to Duarte de Sande, Nanchang, August 29, 1595.[39]

This report to Ricci's superior in Macao documents his progress after leaving Guangdong province as well as his activities in Nanchang, the provincial capital of Jiangxi. The visit in Ji'an is the first description of Ricci in his new guise as a western scholar. The reports on Nanchang focus on his socializing with the elites and his rapidly growing reputation and success, thanks to his books, his command of the Confucian texts, and his knowledge of mathematics and astronomy.

The following day we left Ji'an Prefecture and arrived in a large town in its jurisdiction called Jishui District [Quiexuhien Jishui xian 吉水縣], which could well be a city since this noble and big place, which sits on the right bank of the river, boasts four intendants (*chayuan*) . . . which brings great glory to this town . . . in view that only one such magistrate has come from the entire province of Guangdong. . . . This is also the native place of the magistrate [*zhixian*; Liu Wenfang] of Shaozhou District. We found him here, having just returned a few days ago from his ordinary visit to Beijing that all mandarins have to make at the established time. Since Liu Wenfang was always our friend in Shaozhou—and since he soon had to return there—I decided to pay him a visit. As we had already decided to abandon the name of Buddhist monks . . . and take the name of literati. . . . we have grown our beards and hair down to our ears, and at the same time we have to wear a particular garment, which the literati use during visits; we no longer wear the clothes we wore before as monks. This is the first place we visited this mandarin with beards and dressed like this. . . . Now we are all treated differently from before . . . and I explained to Liu Wenfang our change in garments and that we had abandoned shaving our heads, saying that our profession is letters and that we teach the

39. Source: *Matteo Ricci, Lettere (1580–1609)*, edited by Francesco D'Arelli (Macerata: Quodlibet, 2001), pp. 197–257.

law of God and other things we know. Neither speaking [Chinese] nor understanding the customs of China when we first arrived in Zhaoqing, we were mistaken in dressing as Buddhist monks, from whom we are totally different and opposite, since we hold different doctrines and profess other things.

. . . In this city [Nanchang] there is a famous physician called Wang Jilou. . . . After learning this I decided to gain his friendship. . . . With the friendship of the doctor and of these men [Ming feudatory princes] my reputation began to grow in the city.

* * *

My fame spread [here]. . . . Another mandarin, who is in retirement, on learning that in the city there was a foreigner about whom much was being said, and being fearful of some novelty, went to the *dutang* [Supreme Commander, Lu Wan'gai] and told him about my arrival here, asking him to look into my background in order to find out who I was and what I was up to. . . . [The doctor] came and told me the *dutang* wished to meet me the following day. I went and entered through the door. . . . He asked me different things about virtue and the doctrines we hold, as well as mathematics and the technique for making clocks . . . and he told me he wished me to make him a sundial and an astrolabe.

* * *

Among the important people in this city is a great scholar, Zhang [Huang], whom everyone calls Old Sir Zhang. He has written almost thirty volumes of various books that have been printed, among them some that are considered very erudite; and he is very esteemed and considered a person of good conduct, and a great preacher and master of the doctrine of the literati [Confucians], which is very similar to ours because there is nothing about [Buddhist] beliefs and [it] only treats virtues and ethics in this life. . . .

[With] Sir Zhang and his disciples I already had some debates that left them surprised, since they saw me argue so well using doctrine and arguments taken from their own books. One day, Sir Zhang—seeing himself cornered on the doctrine that I had illustrated concerning paradise and hell, which they deny, holding nothing dear but moral virtues and the good of this life—became embarrassed and said he had nothing more to say about this doctrine except for the words written by a scholar of old: "If there is paradise, good men will ascend there; if there is hell, bad people will descend there. Let's try to be good people, and not evil ones." With this sentence, our dispute came to an end for the time being.

Document 16

Translations from *On Friendship*, the first Chinese work written by Ricci in Nanchang (excerpts).[40]

Ricci's first work in Chinese, a booklet consisting of one hundred maxims on friendship, was quickly written during the first months of his residence in Nanchang. The occasion for its composition is explained by Ricci in the preface. The maxims reflect both a general wisdom about friendship that is equally valid for the West and the East as well as stories from Herodotus and Plutarch that Ricci culled from his memory. The juxtaposition of the familiar (general maxims) and exotic (western exemplars) reflects the friendship between Ricci himself (a virtuous scholar) and the Chinese elites.

Preface

Thus it was that I went to visit the Prince of Jian'an Commandery. I am grateful that he did not despise me but permitted me to greet him with a deep bow. He sat me in the place of the honored guest, and there was much wine and merriment. Then, the prince came over to me, took my hands in his, and said: "Whenever there is a traveler who is a gentleman of virtue who deigns to visit my realm, I have never failed to host him and to treat him with friendship and respect. The nations of the Far West are nations of virtue and righteousness. I wish that I could hear what their discourses on the way of friendship are like." I, Matteo, thus withdrew into seclusion, and from the sayings of old that I had heard since my youth, I compiled this Way of Friendship in one volume, which I respectfully present as follows.

Maxim 18

Only when our virtue and ambitions are alike will a friendship be solid.

---

40. Source: Matteo Ricci, *On Friendship: One Hundred Maxims for a Chinese Prince*, translated by Timothy Billings (New York: Columbia University Press, 2009). I have slightly modified Billings' translations.

Maxim 26

The stability of a friendship is both tested and revealed by the instabilities of my life.

Maxim 27

If you would become my true friend, then love me out of affection; do not love me for material things.

Maxim 92

King Alexander hoped to make friends with a wise scholar named (Shan nuo) Phocion, and sent ahead a messenger to present him with a gift of several tens of thousands in gold. Phocion angrily said: "If the king would bestow gifts like this upon me, what kind of person must he think I am?" The messenger replied: "No, Master, it is not so. The king knows you to be incorruptible. That is why he offers this." To which he answered: "If this is so, then I will also maintain the appearance of my incorruptibility." And he indicated that he would not accept it. Historians conclude the story by saying: "The king wanted to buy the friendship of the scholar, but the scholar would not sell it."

Document 17

Excerpt from *Della entrata* on Ricci's debate with the Buddhist abbot Xuelang Hong'en in Nanjing, 1599.[41]

Li Ruzhen invited Ricci to a banquet. When Ricci and Qu showed up, they found some twenty to thirty invitees at Li Ruzhen's house. The guest of honor was the most famous Buddhist cleric in Nanjing, the abbot Xuelang Hong'en, with the name of San Huai (his secular name was Huang Hong'en). At the time when Hong'en met Ricci, in March/April of 1599, he stood at the apex of his reputation. A brilliant speaker, Hong'en had given lectures on Buddhist texts for thirty years. An expert on the Huayan Sutra, Hong'en enjoyed an enormous reputation as a great Buddhist intellectual, who understood the ideas of intercausality and the interpenetration of all phenomena, the difficult central concepts in the Huayan school. Li Ruzhen had obviously invited Abbot Hong'en to teach Ricci the doctrines of Buddhism.

The father [Ricci] showed up ready for the debate and Li Ruzhen was ready as well, with a famous preacher of the sect of idols, a *heshang* [Buddhist monk], leader of many priests of the idols, who were his disciples, in addition to an infinite multitude of seculars of both sexes. His name was San Huai, and he differed from the other Buddhist clerics in being a great poet, intelligent, and learned in the doctrines of all the sects. . . . He began to indicate that he wanted to speak about religion with the father. The father replied: "Before we discuss anything, I would like you to tell me what you think of the first principle, the creator and lord of heaven and earth and of all created things, whom we call the Lord of Heaven."

San Huai explained: "Yes, there is indeed such a creator of heaven and earth, but he is not a great being, for all human beings are equal to him."

The father asked whether San Huai could do the same things as this creator of heaven and earth? If not, it was just empty talk! San Huai replied yes, that he could create heaven and earth. The father interrupted:

---

41. Source: *Fonti Ricciane*, edited by Pasquale D'Elia (Rome: La Libreria dello Stato, 1942–49), vol. 2, pp. 75–80.

86   *Document 17*

"I don't want to burden you with creating another heaven and earth. I pray you, just create another fire-pot like the one here." San Huai began shouting that this should not be asked of him. The father also began to raise his voice over him, saying he should not have promised something he could not do.

* * *

San Huai started with the beginning of his fantasy; with a great deal of pompous arrogance he asked the father whether he knew mathematics, having heard that he was a great astronomer.

The father replied he knew something about this science, and San Huai added: "When you speak about the sun and the moon, do you go above to the heavens, where the planets stand, or do these planets come down to your heart?" The father said: "I do not go up to heaven, nor do the stars come down to earth. When we see something, we form a figure and species of the thing we have seen in our soul. Afterwards, when we want to think and speak of it, we look inside our own minds at these images we have formed." Hong'en stood up and exclaimed: "Here, just as you yourself have created anew the sun and the moon, you can therefore create all other things." . . . The father explained that "the images in the mind are not the sun and the moon; they are only figures, and are very different from the sun and the moon. And if one has not first seen the sun and the moon, one would not have been able to form these images, not to mention creating the sun and the moon."

He gave him the example of the mirror, in which is reflected the figure of the sun and the moon, when it is positioned in front of them; yet, nobody would be so silly to say that the mirror can create the sun and the moon and the other objects that one can see reflected in it.

[The banquet began.] All the invited guests went to sit down at the tables, which were many. As a foreigner, Ricci was given the place of honor. In the middle of the banquet the literati turned to a much discussed subject in the schools of China: whether human nature is intrinsically good, evil, or indifferent. They say, if it is good, where does the evil come from? And if it is bad, where does good come from? And if it is neither good nor bad, who teaches it to do evil or good, which it does by itself? And since they don't know logic, nor the distinction between moral and natural goodness, what is acquired and what is innate in human nature, still less the corruption of human nature by original sin, and the assistance and grace of God, this question remains open to this day. . . .

The father remained silent all this time without saying anything, and it seemed that many thought he did not understand this question because it is too subtle, or had not paid heed to what was being said; and all wanted to hear him speak about something. At this, he gave a sign that he wished to speak. Everyone fell silent and turned to him with full attention.

First, the father summarized everything the opposing parties had said regarding the good or evil in human nature, which stunned everyone. Then he added: "Nobody can doubt that the Lord of Heaven and Earth is of the highest good. If human nature is so feeble that one doubts whether it is good or evil, how can Master San Huai just now say that human nature is the same as that of God, the creator of heaven and earth? Who can doubt whether that [divine] nature is good or evil?"

* * *

All of Nanjing spoke about this dispute. . . . [And it was said that] the father debated the famous Buddhist monk and was victorious.

Document 18

Letter by the Chinese dissident and scholar Li Zhi to a friend, in which he describes his impressions of Ricci (ca. 1599).[42]

An independent mind, a sharp pen, and an iconoclastic persona made Li Zhi one of the best known and most notorious intellectuals of the Late Ming. These were possibly some of the same qualities that he saw in the exotic western scholar Ricci.

You asked about Ricci: he is a Westerner from the Extreme West, and traveled for over one hundred thousand *li* to reach China, sailing at first to south India, where he first learned of Buddha.... When he reached Guangzhou and the South Sea, he found out that our Great Ming Realm has had the virtuous kings Yao and Shun, and the sages Zhou and Confucius. He lived in the south and in Zhaoqing nearly two decades, reading every book of our nation, asking teachers to help him note the pronunciations and meanings of the words ... so that now he is fluent in speaking and writing our language, and following our rituals. He is a most urbane person. He is a most complex man (*zhong ji linglong*). Very plain and modest in his exterior; and listening to scores of people debating noisily, he can follow and recapitulate their arguments in order. I have never seen anyone more impressive. People are either too critical or too flattering, either showing off their brilliance or coming across as too dull. But I have no idea why he is here. I have met him three times already and still do not know his intention in coming here. Perhaps he wants to use his teachings to change our Confucian learning, but surely that would be silly, and must not be the case.

---

42. Source: Li Zhi in *Xu fen shu* (Book to Be Burned: Sequel), *juan* 1, in *Li Zhi wen ji: Fen shu, xu fen shu* (Beijing: Yan shan chu ban she, 1998), p. 378.

Document 19

Poem dedicated by Li Zhi to Ricci.[43]

[title] Dedicated to Li Xitai [Ricci of the Extreme West]

Leisurely descending from the Northern Darkness,[44]
marching with pleasure toward the South,
like the Kshatriya you leave your name,[45]
recording the maritime journey from the Immortal Island.
Behind your head lie one hundred thousand *li*
as you gaze at the city with nine walls.
Have you seen the light of the country?
The midday sun is shining brilliantly.

---

43. Source: Li Zhi, *Fen shu, juan* 6, p. 301–2. See Haun Saussy, "Matteo Ricci the Dao-ist," chapter 7, pp. 176–93, in *Cross-Cultural Studies: China and the World. A Festschrift in Honor of Professor Zhang Longxi*, edited by Qian Suoqiao (钱锁桥) (Leiden: Brill, 2015).

44. Saussy points out that this is a reference to Zhuangzi (Master Zhuang [ca. 369–286 BCE], who was one of the two central figures in classical Daoist philosophy), and that Ricci is compared to the Monstrous Kun Fish and Peng Bird who migrates from pole to pole, bringing leisure and liberation (*xiaoyao*) to those he encountered by the knowledge he revealed, like the beasts in Zhuangzi who brought enlightenment to those limited in their visions of the universe.

45. The warrior caste of India is both a wordplay on Ricci's Chinese surname, Li, and that of the Kshatriya in Chinese, and also a reference to the fact that the Jesuits first presented themselves in China as monks from India.

Document 20

The Nanjing writer Gu Qiyuan's description of Ricci (ca. 1598–99).[46]

A native of Nanjing, Gu recorded many amusing and interesting anecdotes in his collection of essays, Leftover Conversations from the Guest Seat *(Ke zuo zhui yu). His reminiscence of Ricci reflects the two key attractions of the West that the Jesuit represented: western books and printing, and the techniques of western art.*

[Li Madou, i.e. Ricci, was a] European from the Western oceans. He has a pale face, a curly beard, and deep-seated eyes the color of bright yellow like a cat; he knows Chinese. He came to Nanjing and resided to the west of Zheng Yang Gate, telling everyone the way [*dao*] of his country is the worship of *Tianzhu*, the Lord of Heaven. This *Tianzhu* is the creator of heaven and earth. In painting, it is depicted as a little boy held by a woman, called *Tianmu* [heavenly mother]. This painting was done on a copper board, and the figures look alive, with the bodies, arms, and hands raised above the board; the concaves and declines on the faces make them no different from real people. People ask: "How do you paint this?" He replies: "In Chinese painting, one paints the visible (*yang*) but not the invisible (*yin*), therefore, the human figures look flat, without contrast. The painting of my country uses both yin and yang techniques, and therefore you have contrasts in the faces and roundness in arms and hands. For the human face, if it faces the light, it is painted bright and white; if it faces sideways, the side facing the light is white, whereas the eyes, ears, nose, and mouth that do not face the light are painted dark. The figure painters of my country understand this method, and can therefore erase the distinction between painted figures and real people." He has brought many printed books from his country, all printed on white paper on both sides, with words running horizontally. The paper is like the cotton paper from Yunnan nowadays, thick and sturdy, and the ink is very

---

46. Source: Gu Qiyuan, *Ke zuo zhui yu* (Leftover Conversations from the Guest Seat) (Nanjing: Feng huang chu ban she, 2005), pp. 217–18.

fine. Sometimes there are illustrations, which are fine as hair, of people and buildings. The binding is like the Song folded style, with lacquered leather on the outside for protection, whereas the edges are lined with gold, silver, or copper, and the pages are painted with gold both on the top and bottom. You open the book, and every page looks new; you close the book, and it looks like a plate painted in gold. There is a self-sounding clock, built out of iron, wound with wires, hung up with wheels turning up and down incessantly, and sounding the times. There are many similar instruments, all finely fabricated. . . . He has written *Tianzhu shiyi* and *shilun* [(Ten Discourses); this refers most likely to Ricci's *Jiren shipian* (Ten Discourses of the Man of Paradox)] with many novel sayings, but is most skilled in astronomy and mathematics.

Document 21

Excerpt from *Della entrata* on Ricci's 1600 journey to Beijing and his imprisonment by the eunuch Ma Tang.[47]

During the reign of Wanli, the passivity of the emperor allowed eunuchs in the inner court to amass power. Distrustful and resentful of his mandarins, Wanli also relied on eunuchs to collect salt and mining taxes, which were hugely unpopular in the country. In charge of the Linqing section of the Grand Canal, the eunuch Ma Tang intercepted the boat carrying the Jesuits, craving an opportunity to intercede on behalf of these "tribute-bearing foreigners" and thus enrich himself. A first memorial to the imperial court remained unanswered, and after several months, Ma Tang lost patience with the westerners.

One day, all of a sudden, Ma Tang arrived with the Military Intendant . . . and his entire court, like assassins, numbering about two hundred persons. He said angrily to Ricci that he had received written notice from Beijing that there were many precious stones that Ricci did not want to give to the emperor and that Ricci was also hiding many persons in his household. The father said this was false, as Ma Tang could see with his own eyes; so Ma Tang ordered everything to be brought into the courtyard and gathered everybody around. He then opened all the chests and writing cabinets with great fury and confusion, wanting to examine everything in detail. . . .

The thing that astonished everyone the most and caused us the greatest trouble was that among our things a beautiful crucifix was found: it was carved out of wood and vividly painted the color of blood. The cruel eunuch began to shout and said: "This is a fetish that you have made to kill our emperor! Good people do not travel around with these kinds of objects." He really thought this was an evil thing.

Father Matteo did not want to say this was our God, in part because it was difficult to explain to such ignorant people and in such a delicate

---

47. Source: *Fonti Ricciane*, edited by Pasquale D'Elia (Rome: La Libreria dello Stato, 1942–49), vol. 2, book 4, chapter 11, pp. 115–16.

moment the great mystery, since it would appear to the eunuch that everything said would be an excuse for the evil Ricci had committed; and in part because all eyes were turned on him, full of indignation for the cruelty that seemed to them to have been inflicted on this man [Christ]. For this reason Ricci began to explain slowly to the Military Intendant and others that "they could not even imagine what that thing was; that this was a great saint in our land who wanted to suffer for us the pain of the cross. For this reason we painted and sculpted it in such a way in order to have it always before our eyes and to give thanks for his grace." Nevertheless, the Military Intendant said, it did not seem right to him to have a human figure like this.

Document 22

The mandarin Feng Yingjing's endorsement of Ricci's *True Meaning of the Lord of Heaven* (1603).[48]

A fierce and undaunted critic of the corruption of the eunuchs, Feng was dismissed from office and sent to Beijing for imprisonment. His reputation eventually won him a pardon, but while he was in confinement, Feng was visited by Ricci, whose publications had come to the righteous official's attention some years back. The two men became close friends in a short time. Finding in Christian doctrine and Stoicism wisdom for his troubled country, Feng wrote a preface for Ricci's major work.

Tianzhu shiyi is the dialogue between Ricci of the Great West, his companions and fellow countrymen (及其鄉會友), and us Chinese. Who is the Lord of Heaven, *Tianzhu*? He is *Shangdi*, the God on high, a real and not an empty being. The four great sages, our six Confucian classics, and assorted sages all say: "fear God on high," "help God on high," "serve God on high, and "investigate God on high"; who can say there is anything empty about this? The discourse of emptiness came from India during the reign of Emperor Ming of the Han dynasty. The saint mentioned by Confucius was this Buddha, so those who love novelties claimed; and they so inflated their talk as if Buddha was higher than our *Six Classics*. They were ignorant that India lies to the west of China, and to the west of India is the Great West. In the West, the Buddhists plagiarized some vulgar expressions of Pythagoras and turned them into [the concept of] reincarnation; in China, they stole the idea of an amoral universe from Laozi and turned it into *samsara.* . . .

In antiquity the weary would invoke Heaven, and now they invoke Buddha. In antiquity, people made offerings to heaven, earth, the temple of the state, mountains, rivers, and ancestors, and now to Buddha. In antiquity, scholars knew and obeyed heaven; now they recite Buddhist

48. Source: Zhu Weizheng, editor, *Li Madou zhong wen zhu yi ji* (Shanghai: Fu dan da xue chu ban she, 2001), pp. 97–98.

prayers to become Buddhas.[49] In antiquity, officials diffused reverentially the work of heaven to bring benefits to the people of heaven, not daring to indulge in their own leisure; now great hermits reside at the imperial court, escaping the world in Chan meditation. Who is Buddha but the national teacher of India? Our country has its own national teachers: the three rulers, the five emperors, the three kings, the Duke of Zhou, Confucius, and our own Taizu emperor. Their national teacher insults heaven and puts himself above it; our national teachers follow the commands of heaven and lead the people underneath. If their country follows him, I have nothing to say. But why should we abandon what we have learned and followed [so far]? . . .

This book cites many passages from our *Six Classics* to support the real substance of its arguments, and profoundly criticizes the error of the discourse of emptiness, thus using the West to correct the West, using Chinese culture to reform Chinese culture. The so-called "abandoning of human relations and rejection of the world"—what is vulgarly called "purity from pollution"—is necessary to escape reincarnation, and this clearly shows the absurdity of [the concept of] reincarnation itself. It argues clearly for the cultivation of the self, the expansion of civilization, the respect for filial piety, and the respect for the common ultimate father. It states that human nature is greatly different from that of animals; it advocates that all learning should begin with curbing desire and end in cultivating humanity. It contains things unbeknownst to our country or not yet put into practice. Sir Li [Ricci] has traveled for eighty thousand miles and investigated the nine heavens and nine abysses most accurately. The natural phenomena that we have not profoundly investigated, he has demonstrated with proof, and therefore we ought to accept his reasoning on divinity.

---

49. 作佛 to become or be a Buddha; to cut off illusion, attain complete enlightenment, and end the stage of bodhisattva discipline.

Document 23

Excerpt from Ricci's *True Meaning of the Lord of Heaven* (1603) to illustrate the concordance between Christian moral teachings and Confucian texts and Ricci's attacks on Buddhism.[50]

Set in the form of a dialogue between a western and a Chinese scholar, True Meaning of the Lord of Heaven *resembles in format and style Renaissance humanist writings rather than Chinese philosophical works. Ricci had two aims in the book: to demonstrate the concordance between the ancient Confucian texts and the doctrines of Christianity, and to argue against the teachings of Buddhism. The excerpts selected below represent his attack on a core Buddhist belief: karma, that is, the consequences of one's actions in this and the next life, which inspires the belief in reincarnation, non-killing, and vegetarianism.*

Book 1, Sections 21–23

The Western scholar says: This doctrine about the Lord of Heaven is not the doctrine of one man, one household, or one state. All the great nations from the West to the East are versed in it and uphold it. That which has been taught by sages and worthies has been handed down, from the creation of heaven and earth, men, and all things by the Lord of Heaven, to the present times through canonical writings and in such a manner as to leave no room for doubt. But the scholars of your esteemed country have seldom had contact with other nations, and are therefore unable to understand the languages and culture of our regions and know little of their peoples.

---

50. Source: Matteo Ricci, *The True Meaning of the Lord of Heaven*, translated by Douglas Lancashire and Peter Hu Kuo-chen (St. Louis: Institute of Jesuit Sources, 1985). Used with permission: © The Institute of Jesuit Sources at the Institute for Advanced Jesuit Studies, Boston College, Chestnut Hill, MA. All rights reserved.

I shall explain the universal teaching of the Lord of Heaven in order to prove that it is the true teaching. But before I talk about the number of those who believe in it and their goodness or about what the canonical writings have to say, I shall first present the principles upon which it is based.

Of all things which mark off all men as being different from animals, none is greater than the intellect. The intellect can distinguish between right and wrong and between that which is true and that which is false, and it is difficult to deceive it with anything which lacks rationality. The stupidity of animals is such that although they possess perception and are capable of motion in much the same ways as men, they are incapable of understanding the principles of causality.

Book 5, Sections 263, 280, 282

The Western scholar says: There is so much that is unreasonable in the theory of reincarnation that I would not be able to give you an exhaustive account of it. I shall simply refer to four or five major points, and you will see what I mean.

* * *

Sixth. The rules forbidding the taking of life are due to the fact that people are fearful lest the oxen and horses they slaughter are later incarnations of their parents, and they cannot bear to kill them. But if this is the case, how can they bear to yoke oxen to the plough to till their fields, or to harness them to carts? How can they bear to place a halter on a horse and ride on it? In my view, there is not too great a difference between the crime of killing one's relations and the crime of making them labor in the fields.

* * *

To believe that the human soul can be transformed into another person implies there must be hindrances to marriage and to the use of servants. Why? Who can tell whether the woman you take to be your wife is not a reincarnation of your mother who has become a daughter in a household of a different name? Who can tell whether the servant you use and the underling you abuse is not the reincarnation of your brother, relative, sovereign, teacher, or friend? Is this not again to introduce great confusion into the rules governing human relations?

Document 24

Ricci's World Map compared with a Chinese map of the Ming dynasty and a Portuguese map of 1502.

A world map first prepared by Ricci (see Document 10) and sub-sequently revised and reprinted, contributed significantly to the success of the Jesuit enterprise. The third map below is the 1602 version of Ricci's World Map drawn in Beijing; it measures 192 by 346 centimeters and is found today in the Nanjing Museum. The great strides in European cartography and geography are manifest when we compare it to the first map, the Consolidated Map of the Great Ming, drawn in 1389 under imperial orders and measuring 386 by 456 centimeters. In addition to physical features it represents the administrative units of the realm (districts, counties, and military garrisons). Ming maritime voyages under Zheng He (1405–33) did not bring about any major cartographic advances in China; aside from geographical accounts of foreign lands and detailed sea charts, no extant Ming dynasty maps represent the world beyond East, Southeast, and parts of South Asia. The second map, called the Cantino planisphere (or Cantino World Map), is the earliest surviving map showing Portuguese maritime discoveries in Asia, Africa, and the Americas. It is named after Alberto Cantino, an agent for the Duke of Ferrara in Italy, who successfully smuggled it out of Portugal in 1502. The map is particularly notable for portraying a fragmentary record of the Brazilian coast, discovered by the Portuguese in 1500, and for depicting the African coast of the Atlantic and Indian Oceans with a remarkable accuracy and detail. Note the lack of information on China, since the map was made before the first Portuguese voyage into the South China Sea in 1512.

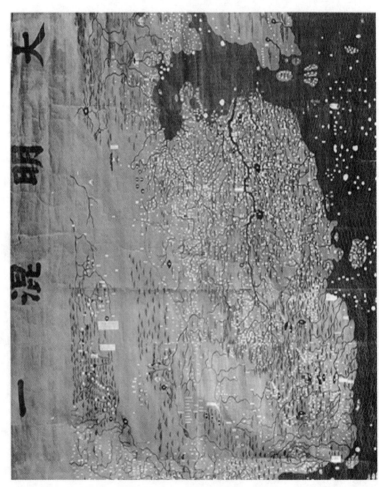

Consolidated Map of the Great Ming, 1389.

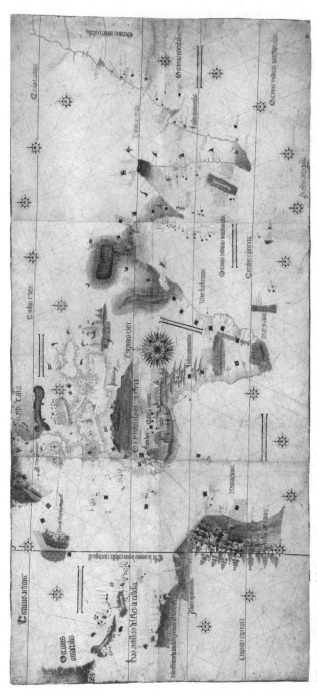

The Cantino World Map, 1502.

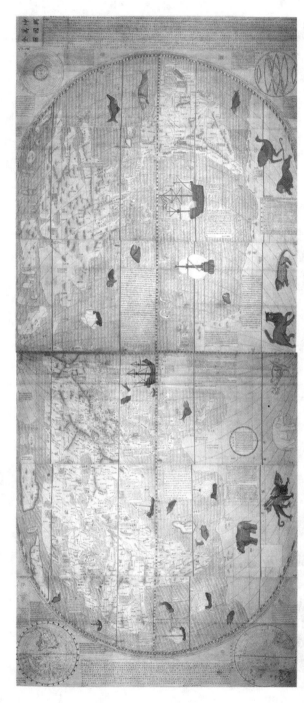

World Map, Matteo Ricci, 1602.

Voyages of St. Francis Xavier

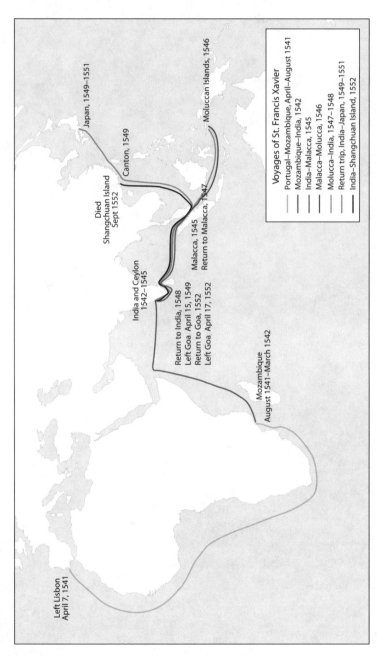

Japan, 1549–1551

Canton, 1549

Died
Shangchuan Island
Sept 1552

Moluccan Islands, 1546

India and Ceylon
1542–1545

Malacca, 1545
Return to Malacca, 1547

Return to India, 1548
Left Goa April 15, 1549
Return to Goa, 1552
Left Goa April 17, 1552

Mozambique
August 1541–March 1542

Left Lisbon
April 7, 1541

Voyages of St. Francis Xavier
Portugal–Mozambique, April–August 1541
Mozambique–India, 1542
India–Malacca, 1545
Malacca–Molucca, 1546
Molucca–India, 1547–1548
Return trip, India–Japan, 1549–1551
India–Shangchuan Island, 1552

Voyages of St. Francis Xavier. For information on Xavier's travels, see page 6.

Document 25

Letter by Ricci to his father, Giovanni Battista Ricci, May 10, 1605.[51]

Ricci's letters to friends in the Society and to his family showed the private side of Ricci, who allowed himself to reveal moments of sadness, disappointment, and longing. Only four family letters written by Ricci are extant and none that are addressed to him. This letter was the last extant letter sent to his father.

Much honored Father in Christ, may the grace and peace of Jesus Christ always be with our souls. Amen.

In the past I have received your letters yearly; and if my letters arrived safely, you also will have news of me, which I can say is good. . . . Things are progressing at the same pace, improving day by day. I am in the court of Beijing, quite close to the Tartars, and will probably be here until I die. . . . There are already more than one thousand Christians. . . . Great is the devotion of the new Christians at mass, sermons, and other festivals of the Church, to which they come frequently and from afar. There is an old man of seventy-two who comes to all the feast days, walking three to four *millia* [ca. 2.5 miles], sometimes in the rain and snow . . . the other day a catechumen seventy-seven years old came to our residence with a bunch of bronze and wooden idols, and some [idols] painted on paper, and books of that sect, so that we could burn and tear them all up, to the great delight of the Christians. . . . A schoolmaster together with seven or eight students became Christians. Another student who is thirteen years old also wanted to become Christian, but the schoolmaster said he was not ready. But one day lightning struck him, and he remained unconscious for three days. During that time he saw God, whose image he had worshipped at school although he was not Christian, and which said to him that this time he would spare his life. And so the schoolmaster prayed for him; the boy recovered and became a Christian, and all Christians call

---

51. Source: *Matteo Ricci, Lettere (1580–1609)*, edited by Francesco D'Arelli (Macerata: Quodlibet, 2001), pp. 389–93.

him Michele of the Lightning. Our Lady appeared to another Christian after he became very ill. She was dressed in white, holding a baby in her arms, with an old man next to her; and Our Lady said to the old man: "Make this man sweat and he will recover." He sweated and immediately felt better, and now he is healthier than ever. . . . I do not have time to relate all the things that have happened, only these few for your consolation.

My task consists of continuously making and receiving visits to and from gentlemen who come in an uninterrupted stream to ask about our faith and our science. Every day I teach one, two, and sometimes three lessons for Jesuits, who are learning Chinese characters, or to those from outside who want to learn our science. I preach on Christian feast days, and I always try to write something in Chinese.

* * *

I do not know where my letter will find you, whether in heaven or on earth; in any case I have wanted to write to you. And now, at the end, remember me to all my kin and friends, whom I have not named because there are so many, but all of whom I remember.

Your most obedient son in Christ
Matteo Ricci

Document 26

Preface by Ricci on the Chinese translation of Euclid and on his collaboration with Xu Guangqi (1608).[52]

Xu Guangqi was one of the most important converts of the Late Ming, rising to the position of Grand Secretary, the highest mandarin office, the year before his death in 1633 (long after Ricci). A strong supporter of Ricci in Beijing, Xu was very interested in introducing western science and technology into China. His collaboration with Ricci in translating the first books of the Greek mathematician Euclid, a foundational authority in western and Arabic mathematics, illustrates the translation method adopted by Ricci and subsequent generations of Jesuit writers to achieve an impressive production of Chinese works.

Since my arrival in China, I have seen that there are many scholars and works on geometry, but I have not seen any fundamental theoretical works. . . . I had then entertained the wish to translate this book for the use of the gentlemen of our times, in order to thank them for their trust in a traveler. Nevertheless, I am of little talent. Moreover, the logic and rhetoric of East and West are so supremely different. In searching for synonyms, there are still many missing words. Even if I can explain things orally with an effort, to put it down in writing is extremely difficult. Ever since then, I have met colleagues who assisted me left and right to advance, but whenever there is a difficulty I would stop, advancing and stopping thrice already. . . .

In 1601, to offer tribute [to the emperor], I lodged in Beijing. In the winter of 1604, Sir Xu [Guangqi] of Jiangsu arrived. An erudite scholar and a great stylist, he has befriended us sojourners for a while; and I thought to myself that with his help, it would not be difficult to translate this book. . . . In the spring he was appointed to the Hanlin Academy . . . in the autumn he inquired about the academies and studies in the West, and

52. Source: Zhu Weizheng, editor, *Li Madou Zhong wen zhu yi ji* (Shanghai: Fu dan da xue chu ban she, 2001), pp. 301–2.

I told him about natural philosophy. When we got to geometry [Euclid], I gave him the gist of its brilliance and explained the difficulties of translation and how I had interrupted my work. Sir Xu said: "Our sages have a saying: the literati (*ru*) should be ashamed if they come across anything they do not know. This one learning has been lost, and all those who wish to know are now searching in the dark. With this book, and with you, Sir, who is neither arrogant nor selfish, I wish to learn. How dare I fear the labor and waste away the days and lose this again in our time? Huh! I avoid difficulties and they grow; I meet them head on and they vanish; we must complete this work." Sir Xu got to work and asked me to discourse orally, and he wrote it down. Pondering and searching words in the Chinese language to represent accurately the meaning of the book, we revised it three times. Sir Xu was so diligent that I dared not slacken. By early spring this year, the most important part, the first six books, have been completed.

Document 27

Excerpts from Ricci's Chinese work *Qiren shipian* (Ten Discourses of the Man of Paradox), which recorded actual conversations between Ricci and Chinese interlocutors on Christianity.[53]

In this book, which was published in 1608, Ricci recalled an episode from his time in Shaozhou (1589–94). There, Ricci met a successful merchant who employed some forty workers. Merchant Guo was a devout Buddhist for most of his adult life. Keeping a permanent Buddhist vegetarian fast, Merchant Guo practiced Chan meditation and all Buddhist rituals. Yet, spiritual consolation seemed to have eluded him. Hence, Merchant Guo visited Ricci. His fervent desire to learn things about the afterlife and the soul greatly edified Ricci. After several days of intense catechism, Ricci baptized Guo, giving him the name of Giuseppe. As a former devotee of Chan meditation, Guo was the first Chinese Christian to practice the Spiritual Exercises of Ignatius of Loyola under the guidance of Ricci. Guo stayed with the Jesuits for one month before business recalled him to Nanxiong.

[492] When I used to live in Shaozhou in the southern part of Guangdong, I became friends with a scholar named Guo. Devoted to virtues, he was no ordinary man. One day, he came to me in tears and said: "I came to bid farewell to you Master, as I will not see you ever again!" Surprised, I asked where he was going and he replied: "I am going to die." Startled, I inquired: "You are not yet old, and you are in good health. How do you know your time is up?" Guo explained: "When I was fifty-five, I met an extraordinary man who discoursed about astrology like a god, who told my fortunes and made predictions for the next five years. Although the good things he predicted did not necessarily happen, all the bad things came true. He told me I shall die before the middle of the fourth month

53. Source: Zhu Weizheng, editor, *Li Madou Zhong wen zhu yi ji* (Shanghai: Fu dan da xue chu ban she, 2001), pp. 492–97.

this year. Well, this month I had a dream and saw various bad omens. Hasn't the augury been proved? Alas! Only at sixty do I get a son; now I will die, and who will take care of this crying baby? I am so sad!"

I pitied his error, stomping my foot in frustration and feeling sorry for him, and when he had finished talking, with a big sigh, I told him (in order to console him): "There is nothing more empty and wrong in this world than the predictions of astrologers and the things we see in dreams. But you consider them real and definitive, isn't that foolish?"

Guo countered: "I saw the signs, how can I not believe?"

[*Ricci goes on to explain that, while there might have been coincidences, most predictions were wrong. Good and bad fortunes result from right and wrong acts that fall within our control. Human will is stronger than the stars. To avoid evil, one has to forsake evil and turn to virtue. For those who refused to repent and still hoped to be spared punishments, even if astrologers might allow it, the Lord of Heaven would not consent! Ricci then used the moral teachings of Confucianism to strengthen his point: Did loyal officials and pious sons recoil from death and danger in serving their country and families in crisis, or did they first consult astrologers? Exposing fortune-tellers and astrologers as frauds, Ricci questioned why these men did not enrich themselves first if they were so clairvoyant, instead of preying on the credulity of the ignorant and anxious. Similarly, dreams were absurd; even if a few seemed true, they were not real.*]

[494] Again, Guo said: "In the past I had never believed in astrologers, but all the things predicted by this master during these past five years came true. I don't dare not to believe them. If only one or two of his words corresponded to the truth, it could be a coincidence; but if every word matches reality, how can I say it is just a chance?"

I said: "How sad! Do you know how these misfortunes in the past years came about? He imposed them on you, and you accepted them. If he had told you nothing, or if you had not believed, no misfortune would have happened. So, the fact that you asked him to tell your fortune has caused you misfortune."

Startled, Merchant Guo asked: "Why?"

I said: "After I had come to China, I observed the customs of your great country, and I was very saddened by the credulity in astrology, fortune-telling, and geomancy, and the great damage that these arts inflict on people, without anybody realizing it. . . . But if you are willing to listen to me, I can save your life." To an expectant and eager Guo, I explained that the human heart was the central organ in the body, . . . and the worst affliction on the heart was fear itself. . . . If one believed in predictions of good fortune, one would rejoice, even if rejoicing could not produce the good things of life. However, if one believed in predictions of misfortune, one would worry; and anxiety led to illness, hence fulfilling the prediction. . . . When I am walking I only need a narrow strip of land measuring no wider than eight inches. But if one places a wooden plank eight inches wide in a high place and asks someone to walk on it, he would fall down even if nobody pushes him. . . ."

Guo asked: "In divining the future, can I not rejoice at good omens and fear not the bad? That is why the ancients often resorted to divinations without any harm."

I said: "It is my decision to go for divination or not, but fear is beyond me. Even for saints and sages, it is difficult not to fear death; can common people do that? Therefore, it is better not to pursue divinations. . . . If one says that destiny is above the Lord of Heaven and not decided by him, it is indeed a great error and one's sins are greatly increased. But if it is under the Lord of Heaven and determined by him, it would be a great insult to the Lord of Heaven if lowly men use it to gain small profits and devise tricks to ascertain it. If you cannot tell what is in men's hearts, how can you divine the profound will of God?"

When Guo heard my discourse he came to a deep understanding and thanked me profoundly. "My teacher has truly given me my life back," he said. "If I had not heard your teachings, I would have given up [life] in vain." . . . I led him to the altar, where Guo gave thanks by prostrating himself, and I repeatedly instructed him not to listen to the various ridiculous schools of divinations and geomancy and serve only the orthodox Lord of Heaven with a true heart.

Guo turned out to be fine after he left. Four years later he got another son. He turned eighty last year, healthy as ever.

Document 28

Letter by the Buddhist layman Yu Chunxi to Ricci, in which he criticizes Ricci's opposition to Buddhism (1608).[54]

In 1608, the Buddhist layman and Ming official, a native of Hang-zhou, Yu Chunxi wrote an open letter to Ricci. The occasion was the publication of Ten Discourses of the Man of Paradox. *Yu began his letter by calling himself an "ineloquent person [bu ning] who does not flatter" and expressing his admiration for Ricci, whose erudition had been praised by his fellow literati from Zhejiang: "Although Mr. Li Xitai [Xitai was Ricci's literati name] is not a Chinese, he is a virtuous man, who is also an expert in astronomy and mathematics." Nevertheless, Yu was provoked into answering the Jesuit's relentless attack on Buddhism.*

When I was three, I learned about the teachings of the three saints [Buddha, Laozi, and Confucius], which I have followed my whole life until the present; I cannot do otherwise.

I have heard recently that you, Sir, who hail from the West, look down on Siddhartha: Is this not similar to the people of ancient Lu dismissing Confucius out of familiar contempt? When I read your comparisons of heaven and hell, it seems you have not flipped through the books [of Buddha] and do not understand their meanings. Have you not heard that in the sutra there is a saying, "Entering the hell without end, not leaving at the end of time, only the longevity of heaven determines his passing, and in one day and night it is already one thousand and six hundred human years"? From this, one can reason that there is something you have missed seeing. If you do not understand its mysteries yet rush to attack, how can you penetrate its strong defenses? I dare invite you to peruse the entire Buddhist Canon issued by the emperor, to classify all the points of similarity and difference, to criticize the shortcomings, and

---

54. Source: Zhu Weizheng, editor, *Li Madou Zhong wen zhu yi ji* (Shanghai: Fu dan da xue chu ban she, 2001), pp. 657–58.

then to publish a book and hang it high above the gate of the palace, so that the Buddhist monks with their left chests bared can shoot arrows at will. If no feather should stick to the target, and the archers have emptied their quivers for nothing, wouldn't that be a great historic achievement! But I see you do not do this, saying instead slanderous remarks that make other people laugh behind your back. Have you no better plan? If you are occupied every day with your studies and have no time to peruse all the books [of Buddhism], please start with reading these books: *Zong jing lu* [Record of the Mirror of the (Chan) Lineage],[55] *Jie fa yin* [Exposition on Rules in the Brahman-Net Sutra],[56] *Xi yu ji* [History of the Western Region],[57] *Gao zeng zhuan* [Biographies of Eminent Monks],[58] *Fa yuan zhu lin* [Trees from the Park of Dharma].[59] Find out the subtleties and arguments, if only to begin to offer an apology. Otherwise, if you only say: "My country has always found this person [i.e. Buddha] despicable; and I know everything about his place of birth." How do we know this is not a different western heaven, another Siddhartha? . . . How can one individual's skepticism cast doubt on the faith of thousands? Traveling with white horses to the East and fragrant elephants to the West, preachers and interpreters never ceased their journeys. You can fool one man, but not ten thousand.

How can you say that in more than two thousand years, the numerous saints and sages of our noble China have all been fooled by the doctrines of Buddhism? Let us not denigrate any individual but simply discuss the merits of his books. [The Confucian philosophers] Lu Xiangshan and Wang Yangming have transmitted Buddhist learning, and yet they are honored in Confucian temples;[60] thus we know that Buddhist scriptures are similar to the teachings of neo-Confucianism (*li*). Moreover,

---

55. Composed by Yanshou in the 10th century.

56. This was written by Yu's master, the monk Zhuhong (1535–1615).

57. By Xuanzang (600–664), the most famous Chinese Buddhist monk, who studied in India during the Tang dynasty.

58. First compiled by Huijiao (497–550) with new, revised editions from the Tang, Song, and Ming dynasties.

59. A 7th-century work.

60. Lu Jiuyuan, with the honorary name of Xiangshan (1138–91), and Wang Shouren, with the honorary name Yangming (1472–1529), were the two neo-Confucian scholars who were particularly influenced by Zen Buddhism.

Emperors Taizu and Wenhuang [the first two emperors of the Ming] honored statues of the Buddha. Wise ministers and famous officials defended Buddhism with their might: Is it that easy to use [Han Yu's] words "burn Buddhist sutras and turn their monasteries into homes for the people"?[61] Let us wish it is not the case that when a westerner attacks another westerner, and if he fails, his school will collapse. If the Lord of Heaven (Tianzhu) can manifest his spirit, how can he bear to arm you with armor and weapons to result in the destruction of his holy city and the loss of his blessed territory?

I, the ineloquent, know that you, Sir, honor the commandments of the Lord of Heaven as firmly as metal and stone, and will in no way betray your teacher or friends. While the Confucian classics and the history books are indeed worthy of citation, there are also many places in the Buddhist sutras that are harmonious with your teachings. Yet, without a casual reading, you attack them, whereas those who have read your *Ten Discourses of the Man of Paradox* say: "This is no different from Buddhist teachings!" What you are offering, Sir, are merely wild pigs and celeries![62]

Indeed! All of us living beings exist within the seed of a fruit, ignorant of its peel or its shell, not to mention the things outside of the fruit! Whether this is all the same teaching is for you, Sir, to decide.

Opening my mouth while lying on my pillow, I feel deeply ashamed; may I beg the indulgence of your grand magnanimity for having attacked a foreigner. Your humble servant, your humble servant!

---

61. Han Yu (768–824) was the most prominent official and scholar in the Tang dynasty who opposed Buddhism.

62. This is a reference to two stories of peasants bringing white pigs and celeries to the imperial palace, only to discover that these were not at all rarities. Yu is mocking Ricci for bringing Christian teachings (the wild pigs and celeries), precious only to himself, to China, where Buddhism has already taught these doctrines in great abundance.

Document 29

Excerpts from a letter by Ricci to Francesco Pasio, vice-provincial in the Japan Jesuit mission, February 15, 1609.[63]

In this letter, the penultimate written by Ricci, he sums up his experiences in China and offers judgment on his own work. The political situation in China was such that no one, except for the eunuchs, had access to the emperor (Wanli), not to mention the intricate and complex procedures of the bureaucracy, hence the impossibility for the Jesuits to submit a petition for regularizing their residence. On the other hand, Ricci observed from experience that many things forbidden by the law were in fact tolerated, such as the presence of Muslims and of the Jesuits. Despite many calls for the expulsion of the missionaries, they remained. After analyzing the conditions of the mission, Ricci stated eight factors that would affect Christian evangelization.

[513] Your reverence can imagine from this how it will be humanly impossible to ask for, and obtain, license to preach our law openly, because no mandarin would have wanted to present such a hitherto unheard of memorial in China. Nonetheless, some of our fathers write to me saying I need to obtain such a license. On this I say we are secure and do not require any license. We have already survived numerous petitions, submitted to the mandarins, to have us kicked out of China. . . . I believe this not just because I understand the reasons and customs of this realm, but because we have felt the truth with our own hands. The same will be so, with the grace of God, even after we, the first ones, are dead, or this emperor should die. It seems to me that we have generated a great deal of good credit and good opinion not just among those outside of court, but even with the mandarins of the court, and even if it is not true that the emperor is benevolent or that he will hear us out, we should still put

---

63. Source: *Matteo Ricci, Lettere (1580–1609)*, edited by Francesco D'Arelli (Macerata: Quodlibet, 2001), pp. 509–20.

more fathers in different parts of China . . . until there are enough of us in China not to fear expulsion, by means of which others can enter, every year, albeit clandestinely (as I said) like the sect of the Turks of Persia do all the time, without the Chinese noticing or able to prevent it. For I have not found the law that many say prescribes the death penalty for illegal entry; nor have we ever been threatened with, or accused under, such a law.

Ricci's Summary Reflections

The first thing is to see the miraculous progress we have made since the beginning of this mission. . . . We can already count thousands of Christians, we are at the two courts and in another two important cities, and we enjoy the greatest reputation we have ever had. We converse with the leaders of the realm, and are considered not only men of great virtue but also of learning, the two qualities which are most esteemed here.

Second: since in this realm letters are highly esteemed, and consequently the sciences and rational thought [as well] . . . it will thus be easy to persuade the leaders of the realm that the things of our holy faith are confirmed with rational evidence. With the most important of the leaders agreeing with us, it will be easy to convert the rest of the people.

Third: it follows that we could more easily propagate our holy Christian religion with books that can travel everywhere without hindrance; books reach more people, more often, than we can, and can provide greater detail and precision than we can orally; we know this from experience. Because by means of the four or five books we have published up to now, our holy law and its good reputation have spread much further than before with words and other means. . . . If we can put down exactly in books all the things of our holy faith, the Chinese themselves will spread our holy faith with instructions, and the converts can maintain their faith even though no priests can visit them.

Fourth: the Chinese are by nature intelligent and clever, which can be seen in their books, discourses, in the elaborate clothing they make, and in their governance, which is the envy of all of the Orient. If we can teach them our science, they would not only succeed in being eminent men, but we could also easily induce them to embrace our holy law. . . . Until now, I have taught them nothing except for a bit of mathematics and cosmography . . . and I have often been told, by important people, that we have opened the blind eyes of the Chinese; and they say this only after hearing my teaching on the natural science of mathematics. What would they say if they knew about the more abstract subjects such as physics, metaphysics, theology, and the supernatural?

Fifth: ... From the beginning, in antiquity, the Chinese have followed the natural law more exactly than in our countries. For one thousand and five hundred years this people was little given over to idolatry; and the idols they adored were not as destructive as those adored by our Egyptians, Greeks, and Romans, but rather figures that they thought were virtuous and did good works. As a matter of fact, the books of the literati, which are the most ancient and most authoritative, describe no worship except for that of heaven and earth and its lord. And, having examined well all these books, we find in them little that runs contrary to the light of reason and much in conformity—their natural philosophers second to none—and we can hope that with divine mercy, and through the grace of God's love, many of the Chinese ancients who observed natural law were saved.

* * *

[519] Six: the peace in which this realm has maintained itself for hundreds of years would be useful for preserving the lives of Christians ... and if this peace has lasted until now without the Christian law that has pacified so many discordant ancient realms, how will it be after the introduction of the law of union and of peace? I have seen how this argument has served our Christians by improving the reputation of our law and propagating the belief that if the Chinese were Christians, there would never be rebellions and dynastic changes, which are feared so much.

* * *

Seven: ... through publication of our books and our participation in their rituals, we have all gained the names of learned and virtuous men, and I hope we will continue to be considered so until the end. This is important, because even though there are many learned men and theologians among us here, none of them has achieved even a mediocre command of Chinese letters—and knowing our own language without knowing theirs accomplishes nothing.

* * *

Eight: I want to finish this part by talking about the support our faith has received in the books written by the Chinese literati. Your Reverend knows that there are three sects in this realm: the most ancient, the literati, has always governed China; the other two [Daoism and Buddhism] are idolatrous, in disagreement, and are always combated by the literati. Even if the literati sect does not speak about supernatural things, their ethics are almost entirely in concordance with ours. Thus I began to praise the literati in my books; doing so allowed me to use them to confute the other sects without refuting the Confucian texts, and interpreting places that seem contrary to our holy faith.

Document 30

The legacy of Ricci in China.

To this date, Ricci remains the best known Christian missionary and one of the most famous westerners to have visited China. However, in his own lifetime and in the generation after his death, Ricci was a divisive figure because of his harsh attacks on Buddhism. The four texts below represent this spectrum of opinion, with two representing the Buddhist side, highly critical of Ricci, and two representing the high regard of Ricci's Chinese collaborators and converts. Note the different interpretations of Ricci's accommodation to Confucianism by the two camps.

This first excerpt was written by the Buddhist monk Yunqi Zhuhong (1534–1615), abbot of a famous monastery in Hangzhou. Fiercely critical of lax Buddhist discipline, Zhuhong strove to synthesize Confucian teachings with Buddhism. A master of many lay followers, among whom was Yu Chunxi (see Document 28), Zhuhong was considered one of the four great Buddhist monks of the Late Ming. Zhuhong and Ricci never met.

An old man told me: "There is a foreigner who believes in the Lord of Heaven, why do you not refute him?" "I thought that it is a good thing that he teaches people to respect heaven, why should I refute him?" The old man said: "Because he wants to use this to change our customs and simultaneously to destroy Buddhism and the *dharma*; and many learned literati and good friends believe in him." He showed me [Ricci's book, i.e. *True Meaning of the Lord of Heaven*], and so I will briefly refute it. Even though he worships the Lord of Heaven, he does not really understand this teaching. . . . The Lord of Heaven, whom he calls the highest, is merely a feudal vassal seen from the Buddhist cosmos, just like the emperor of Zhou regarded his thousands of vassals. He only knows one Lord of Heaven among millions, and is ignorant of the different worlds and heavens. . . . He may be intelligent, but it is not surprising his arguments are ridiculous since he had not read the sutras.

Men and women marrying, the use of draft animals and servants: these are common human customs and cannot be compared to the cruelty of killing. Therefore the [*Net*] *Sutra* says it is forbidden to kill any living things, but it does not say we cannot marry or command living things. To raise objections like these is just petty, clever, and useless talk: How can it destroy the clear commandments of the great way?[64]

* * *

This second text was written by Huang Zhen, a Buddhist layman, in the 1630s. A native of Fujian, Huang Zhen met and discussed Christian teachings with the Italian Jesuit Giulio Aleni, who arrived in China in 1611, one year after Ricci's death. Highly hostile to Christianity, Huang Zhen accused the Jesuits of using Confucianism to undermine Buddhism and subvert Chinese culture.

One should really cry and sigh over the fact that no one in the world has opposed the introduction of the heterodox teachings of the Lord of Heaven into China. In the past, only Sir Yu Chunxi [see Document 28] and Monk Lotus Pond [i.e. Zhuhong, see above] have opposed this heterodoxy. Old Monk Lotus Pond said to me: "I will oppose it despite my decrepit body." Regrettably he passed away soon thereafter. At that time, Master Lotus Pond had not met Li Madou [Ricci] face-to-face, was unacquainted with the details of his heterodox teachings, and did not refute him in depth. Moreover, there were only a few Catholic books. . . . Today, there are many such titles . . . circulating everywhere and confusing everyone.

* * *

The fact that Ricci and his gang have come successively to China is nothing but a plan by their whole country to subvert the Chinese with barbarian ways, and to grab the two supreme powers of ruling and teaching. Now their country has secretly studied our language and books, and has obtained the right to emend the calendar; it is a cunning and profound stratagem to select and reward with riches their people who can teach in

---

64. Source: Zhuhong, *Tianshuo* (On Heaven), in *Ming mo Qing chu Tianzhu jiao shi wen xian cong bian* (Beijing: Beijing tu shu guan chu ban she, 2001), 5 vols. Here, vol. 4, 207a–208a.

our realm. Thus, the barbarians devote their entire energy to this. Any doctrine that can subvert the teachings of our holy sages they do not refrain from. . . . It has been more than fifty years from the beginning of this catastrophe with Ricci until today, and none of our literati and scholars have defended Mencius. The image of loyalty, filial piety, and virtue is diminished daily, and the principle of heaven's way and virtuous nature is growing dark. It is truly something to cry and lament.[65]

* * *

On June 10, 1625, Li Zhizao (李之藻), Dr. Leo in the Jesuit sources, published a rubbing of a Tang dynasty Nestorian stele that was recently discovered in Xian. Li also wrote a postscript, Du Jingjiao bei shuhou (讀景教碑書後) [A Postscript after Reading about the Nestorian Stele], in which he narrated the discovery and commented on the text of the stele. Observing perhaps that Nestorian scriptures might have survived in the Buddhist texts, Li comments that since there were doubts about using Confucianism to convey the learning of Heaven, therefore the Nestorians used the name of seng, Buddhist monk. He goes on to remember Ricci.

The reason for this is that in their country [Persia, and the Nestorians] there was no distinction between the clergy and the laity. Their laity did not grow their hair long, and the men wore their hair close-cropped. Thus the Chinese insisted they were Buddhist monks, and they could not explain the difference. Similarly, when Ricci first entered Guangzhou, he hid his identity for many years. Later, he met Qu Taisu who discerned that he was not a Buddhist monk, after which he grew his hair and called himself *ru*, a Confucian scholar. Visiting the imperial capital, he was honored by rituals and benevolence by our Wanli emperor and given a residence where he lived for many years. . . . For thirty years, the gentry and literati of our China have grown familiar with their virtuous doctrines and practices. Is there anyone who does not marvel at and respect them? However, there are believers and doubters, and many among the

---

65. Source: Two anti-Christian works by Huang Zhen, in *Ming mo Qing chu Tianzhu jiao shi wen xian cong bian* (Beijing: Beijing tu shu guan chu ban she, 2001), 5 vols. Here, vol. 3, 149a, 150a–b.

latter criticize it as a new doctrine. Who knew that this religion has been propagated for nine hundred and ninety years![66]

* * *

As a close collaborator and friend of Ricci (see Document 26), Xu Guangqi together with Li Zhizao (see above) were two of the strongest and most influential supporters of the Catholic Church in Late Ming China. Like Li, Xu also wrote a text to commemorate the discovery of the Tang dynasty Nestorian stele, in which he highlights Ricci's achievements.

Our China has known the Lord of Heaven since the arrival of Matteo Ricci, who has offered the holy texts and statues to the imperial court. Awarded a stipend, he began socializing with officials and literati, and from conversations he proceeded to publish his writings and attract many followers. Arriving in the capital in 1600, Ricci has worshiped the holy statues in great reverence, thus attracting many admirers and imitators, especially since the imperial bestowal of a tomb in the year 1611. Knowing the true lord, Ricci traveled alone for ninety thousand *li* to expound his highest teachings, and all men of virtue within the realm flocked to follow, with believers numbering in the thousands. There is one reason why some cannot overcome their doubts: Why? They point to those thoughtless scholars who argue that this teaching has never been heard of in the past. Oh my! If the ancients did not write about it, then creation does not exist? All things in the universe are indeed created. The religion of Heaven has been known in China for more than one millennium and is not newly invented. How do we know this? We know this because in 1623, a Tang dynasty stele was excavated in Shaanxi. . . . And thus it is manifest that this doctrine is harmonious with a prosperous reign, abandoned in times of crisis; it sinks and disappears in times of disorder and anarchy, and shines brightly in days of brilliant rule. Truly, this is the invisible and silent will of the lord and not the doings of man.[67]

---

66. Source: Li Zhizao, "Du Jingjiao bei shuhou," in [Liu Ning (劉凝), ca. 1625–1715, editor], *Tianxue jijie* (天學集解), *juan* 1, 53b. ca. 1660, manuscript, Public Library of Saint Petersburg; copy in Sinological Library, Leiden University, The Netherlands.

67. Source: Xu Guangqi, "Jingjiao tang bei ji," [景教堂碑記] in [Liu Ning (劉凝), ca. 1625–1715, editor], *Tianxue jijie* (天學集解), *juan* 1, 55a–56a.

SELECT BIBLIOGRAPHY

General Overviews

To understand Matteo Ricci, one should start by knowing his world, which encompassed both the Catholic Europe of the Counter-Reformation, Portuguese India, and China in the Late Ming dynasty. The following titles represent selected works that illustrate that world.

Alden, Dauril. *The Making of an Enterprise: The Society of Jesus in Portugal, Its Empire, and Beyond 1540–1750*. Stanford, CA: Stanford University Press, 1996.

The most comprehensive study of the history of the Jesuits in Portugal and its dominions.

Barreto, Luís Filipe. *Macao: Poder e saber, séculos XVI e XVII*. Lisbon: Editorial Presença, 2006.

Represents the current scholarship on the history of early Macao based on Portuguese sources.

Boxer, Charles. *The Church Militant and Iberian Expansion 1440–1770*. Baltimore: Johns Hopkins University Press, 1978.

A succinct and general introduction to the relationship between Catholic missions and the Iberian maritime empires.

Brockey, Liam M. *Journey to the East: The Jesuit Mission to China, 1579–1724*. Cambridge, MA: Harvard University Press, 2007.

A good general overview of the Jesuit Mission under Portuguese patronage that relies on the papers in the Ajuda Library in Lisbon.

Brook, Timothy. *Praying for Power: Buddhism and the Formation of Gentry Society in Late-Ming China*. Cambridge, MA: Harvard University Press, 1993.

Best analysis and overview of Buddhism in the Late Ming.

Delumeau, Jean. *Vie économique et sociale de Rome dans la seconde moitié du XVIe siècle*. 2 vols. Paris: de Boccard, 1957.

Detailed study of the social and economic life of the Papal States and Rome in the second half of the 16th century.

Fan, Shuzhi 樊树志. *Wan li zhuan* 万历传 (Biography of Wanli). Beijing: Ren min chu ban she, 1993.

A lively scholarly study of the reign of Emperor Wanli, with detailed information on some of the mandarins whom Ricci encountered.

Gernet, Jacques. *China and the Christian Impact: A Conflict of Cultures*. Cambridge: Cambridge University Press, 1985.

A controversial book that argues for the fundamental incompatibility between Christian and Chinese cultures.

Guo, Peng 郭朋. *Ming qing fo jiao* 明清佛教 (Buddhism in the Ming and Qing Dynasties). Fuzhou: Fu jian ren min chu ban she, 1982.

A good introduction to the history of Buddhism in Ming-Qing China.

Ollé, Manel. *La invencíon de China: Percepciones y estrategias Filipinas respecto a China durante el siglo XVI*. Wiesbaden: Harrassowitz, 2000.

This well-researched book on early Sino-Spanish relations has interesting information on Alonso Sanchez.

Roscioni, Gian Carlo. *Il desiderio delle Indie: Storie, sogni e fughe di giovani gesuiti italiani*. Turin: Einaudi, 2001.

A study of the letters sent by aspiring Jesuit missionaries from the Italian provinces in the 16th and 17th centuries.

Sun, Shangyang 孙尚扬. *Ji du jiao yu ming mo ru xue* 基督教与明末儒学 (Christianity and Late Ming Confucianism). Beijing: Dong fan chu ban she, 1994.

A pioneering historical-philosophical study of the early encounter between Confucianism and Christianity set in the larger context of Sino-western relations.

Yü, Chün-fang. *Kuan-yin: The Chinese Transformation of Avalokitesvara.* New York: Columbia University Press, 2001.

Definitive study of the cult of Guanyin, often confused with the Virgin Mary by early European visitors to China and by the earliest Chinese converts.

Primary Sources

This section lists the manuscript and published documents pertaining to a study of Matteo Ricci, including his writings in western languages and in Chinese, as well as other documents related to the early Jesuit mission in China.

Aleni, Giulio. *Da Xi Xi Tai Li xian sheng xing ji* 大西西泰利先生行蹟 (The Life of Master Li from the Great West). Taibei Shi: Tai bei li shi xue she, 2002.

The earliest Chinese biography of Ricci, written by the Italian Jesuit Aleni, which incorporates oral traditions at the time of Ricci's death.

Archivum Romanum Societatis Iesu. Jap-Sin 101 I.

This manuscript, written in Michele Ruggieri's hand, contains the memoirs of his years in China, a description of his voyage back to Europe, and other notes.

Billings, Timothy. *On Friendship: One Hundred Maxims for a Chinese Prince.* New York: Columbia University Press, 2009.

Translation of Ricci's first successful Chinese work, published in 1595 in Nanchang and dedicated to a Ming prince.

Boxer, C. R., editor. *South China in the Sixteenth Century.* London: The Hakluyt Society, 1953.

Translation from the Spanish of the narratives of three visitors to China: the soldier Galeote Pereira and the Dominican Gaspar da Cruz, both Portuguese, and the Spanish Augustinian friar Martin de Rada.

Cartas que os padres e irmãos da Companhia de Iesus escreuerão dos Reynos de Iapão e China aos da mesma Companhia da India, e Europa, des do anno de 1549 atè o de 1580. Vol. 2. Evora, 1598. Maia: Castoliva, 1997.

Collection of early reports from the Portuguese Jesuit missions to India, Japan, and China.

Chan, Albert, S.J. "Michele Ruggieri, S.J. (1543–1607) and His Chinese Poems." *Monumenta Serica* 41 (1993): 129–76.

Study and text of classical Chinese poems written by Ruggieri, discovered in the Archivum Romanum Societatis Iesu.

Colin, Francisco. *Labor evangelica: Ministerios Apostolicos de los Obreros de la Compañia de Iesus, fundacion, y progressos de su Provincia en las Islas Filipinas.* Edited by Pablo Pastells. 3 vols. Barcelona: Henrich, 1900–1902.

Collection of the earliest documents concerning Spanish rule in the Philippines, including writings by the Jesuit Alonso Sanchez, which are relevant to the Jesuit mission in China.

De Christiana expeditione apud Sinas: Suscepta ab Societate Jesu ex P. Matthaei Riccii eiusdem Societatis commentariis libri V ad S.D.N. Paulum V in quibus Sinensis Regni mores, leges, atque instituta, et novae illius Ecclesiae difficillima primordia accurate et summa fide describuntur. Augsburg, 1615.

The Latin translation of Ricci's memoirs by the Belgian Jesuit Nicolas Trigault, which contains additions by the latter. This work established the importance of the Jesuit China mission and the reputation of Ricci.

D'Elia, Pasquale, editor. *Fonti Ricciane: Matteo Ricci: Storia dell'introduzione del Cristianesimo in Cina.* 3 vols. Rome: La Libreria dello Stato, 1942–49.

The critical edition of Ricci's memoirs with an extensive apparatus. (Ricci's correspondence remains unpublished.)

De Ursis, Sabatino. *P. Matheus Ricci, S.J.: Relação escripta pelo seu companheiro P. Sabatino de Ursis, S.J.; publicação commemorative do terceiro centenario da sua morte.* Rome: Enrico Voghera, 1910.

The first biography of Ricci written by his Jesuit companion in Beijing present at the time of his death.

Gallagher, Louis J. *The China That Was: China as Discovered by the Jesuits at the Close of the 16th Century.* Milwaukee: Bruce, 1942.

This English translation of the Latin translation by Trigault contains no critical apparatus and makes it impossible to identify Ricci's Chinese interlocutors.

Gu, Qiyuan 顾起元. *Ke zuo zhui yu* 客坐赘语 (Leftover Conversations from the Guest Seat). Nanjing: Feng huang chu ban she, 2005.

These vignettes of life in Nanjing ca. 1600 contain two entries concerning Ricci.

Li, Yuqing 黎玉琴, and Liu, Mingqiang 刘明强. "Li Madou shi hai gou chen yi ze" 利玛窦史海钩沉一则 ("One Case Study from the Historical Research on Matteo Ricci"). *Zhao qing xue yuan xue bao* 肇庆学院学报 (Journal of Zhaoqing College) 32, no. 4 (July 2011): 1–5.

This article provides a rare source on the life of Ricci in Shaozhou during his early years in China. It is a biography by Liu Chengfan, who met Ricci while the Jesuit was still dressed as a Buddhist monk.

Li, Zhi 李贽. *Li Zhi wen ji: Fen shu, xu fen shu* 李贽文集：焚书, 续焚书 (Book to Be Burned; Book to Be Burned, a Continuation). Beijing: Yan shan chu ban she, 1998.

References to Ricci in this collection of writings by the leading nonconformist in Late Ming China.

Liu, Tong 刘侗, and Yu, Yizheng 于奕正, editors. *Di jing jing wu lüe* 帝京景物略 (Scenes and Monuments from the Imperial Capital). Shanghai: Yuan dong chu ban she, 1997.

A guidebook to sights in the imperial capital that contains descriptions of the Catholic Church and residence (Nantang, the Southern Church).

Loureiro, Rui Manuel, editor. *Em busca das origens de Macao (antologia documental)*. Lisbon: Grupo de Trabalho do Ministéro da Educação para as comemorações dos descobrimentos Portugueses, 1996.

Documents concerning the earliest history of Macao, including the role of the Jesuits.

Martin, Gregory. *Roma Sancta*. Edited by George Bruner Parks. Rome: Edizioni di Storia e Letteratura, 1969.

Observations of Roman life and ecclesiastical institutions by a contemporary English priest.

Pantoja, Diego de. *Relacion de la entrada de algunos padres de la Compañia de Iesus en la China, y particulares sucesos que tuvieron, y de cosas muy notables que vieron en el mismos reyno.* Valencia: Juan Chrysostomo Garriz, 1606.

The memoirs by Ricci's first Jesuit companion who traveled with him from Nanjing to Beijing in 1600. There is also a modern edition: Moncó Rebollo, Beatriz, editor. *Relación de la entrada de algunos padres de la Compañía de Jesús en la China y particulares sucesos que tuvieron y de cosas muy notables que vieron en el mismo reino: Carta del Padre Diego de Pantoja, religioso de la Compañía de Jesús, para el Padre Luis de Guzmán, provincial de la Provincia de Toledo.* Alcorcón (Madrid): Instituto de Estudios Históricos del Sur de Madrid «Jiménez de Gregorio», 2011.

Pavur, Claude, S.J., translator. *The Ratio Studiorum: The Official Plan for Jesuit Education.* St. Louis: Institute of Jesuit Sources, 2005.

English translation of the Plan of Studies for Jesuit Colleges.

Ricci, Matteo. *Matteo Ricci: Lettere (1580–1609).* Edited by Francesco D'Arelli. Macerata: Quodlibet, 2001.

The most accessible edition of the letters of Ricci, with Italian translations provided for the Portuguese originals. (For detailed archival descriptions of the materials, see the edition by Tacchi-Venturi, which is, however, much less accessible.)

Ricci, Matteo. *Opere Storiche del P. Matteo Ricci S.I.* 2 vols. Edited by Pietro Tacchi-Venturi. Macerata: F. Giorgetti, 1913.

The first edition of the western writings of Ricci (*Della entrata* and letters). Though this edition of the *Della entrata* has since been superseded by Pasquale D'Elia's edition, it is still useful to consult the letters by other Jesuits included in this volume (D'Elia does not include the letters). The Tacchi-Venturi edition of the *Lettere* is still superior to the D'Elia edition (although the latter has one extra letter discovered later by D'Elia).

Ricci, Matteo. *Tianzhu shiyi: The True Meaning of the Lord of Heaven*. Translated by Douglas Lancashire and Peter Hu Guozhen. St. Louis: Institute of Jesuit Sources, 1985.

Bilingual edition of Ricci's best known work.

Ricci, Matteo, and Trigault, Nicolas. *China in the Sixteenth Century: The Journals of Matthew Ricci: 1583–1610*. New York: Random House, 1953.

A reprint of Gallagher's 1942 translation of Trigault.

Shen, Defu 沉德符. *Wan li ye huo bian* 万历野获编 (Unofficial Recordings from the Wanli Reign). Beijing: Zhong hua shu ju, 2004.

Vignettes and stories of the Wanli reign (1563–1620); contains a few entries concerning Ricci and the Jesuits.

Standaert, Nicolas, and Dudink, Adrian, editors. 耶穌會羅馬檔案館明清天主教文獻 (Chinese Christian Texts from the Roman Archives of the Society of Jesus). 12 vols. Taipei: Ricci Institute, 2002.

Writings by Xu Guangqi and other Chinese converts of the first generation are included.

Tordesillas, Agustín de. *Relación de el viaje que hezimos en China nuestro hermano fray Pedro de Alpharo con otros tres frailes de la orden de nuestro seraphico padre san Francisco de la prouincia de san Joseph etc.* 1578. Archivo de la Real Academia de la Historia, Velázques, tomo LXXV. Available at http://www.upf.edu/asia/projectes/che/s16/tordes.htm (La China en España). Elaboración de un corpus digitalizado de documentos españoles sobre China de 1555 a 1900, p. 13.

This is the description of the Augustinians' voyage from Manila to Guangdong, which includes their interview in Zhaoqing.

Van den Wyngaert, Anastasius, editor. *Sinica franciscana, vol. 2. Relationes et epistolas fratrum minorum saeculi XVI et XVII*. Ad Claras Aquas [Quaracchi-Firenze]: Apud Collegium S. Bonaventurae, 1933.

Collection of letters and reports concerning the Franciscan mission to China.

Wicki, Joseph, editor. *Documenta Indica, 1540–1597.* 18 vols. Rome: Monumenta Historica Societatis Iesu (MHSI), 1948–88.

Collection of documents related to the Jesuit mission in India, including letters by missionaries describing their voyage from Lisbon.

Witek, John. *Dicionário Português-Chinês (Pu Han ci dian; Portuguese Chinese Dictionary).* San Francisco: Ricci Institute for Chinese-Western Cultural History, University of San Francisco; and Lisboa: Biblioteca Nacional Portugal, Instituto Português do Oriente, 2001.

This published edition of the Sino-Portuguese dictionary attributed to Ruggieri and Ricci (a claim disputed by Barreto) includes notes on the Chinese language, geography, and time system. However, the copy of the verdict concerning Ruggieri's trial of adultery is unfortunately left out by the editor.

Witek, John W., and Sebes, Joseph S., editors. *Monumenta Sinica, vol. I (1546–1562).* Rome: Institutum Historicum Societaties Iesu IIHSI), 2002.

Excerpts of the earliest Jesuit documents related to the Society's China mission.

Zhu, Weizheng 朱维铮, editor. *Li Madou zhong wen zhu yi ji* 利玛窦中文著译集 (Collection of Chinese Writings and Translations by Matteo Ricci). Shanghai: Fu dan da xue chu ban she, 2001.

This edition of Ricci's Chinese works collects, in one volume, all his writings in that language.

Ricci and His World Map

One of Ricci's most successful "publications" was his adaptation of a world map published by the Antwerp printer Abraham Ortelius. With Chinese nomenclature and annotations added to the large-format map, the *Mappamondo* was a sensation in Late Ming China and exerted a significant influence on the development of Chinese geographic knowledge.

Chen, Guansheng 陳觀勝. "Li Madou dui zhong guo di li xue zhi gong xian ji qi ying xiang"「利瑪竇對中國地理學之貢獻及其影響」("The Contributions and Influence of Matteo Ricci to Chinese Geography"). *Yu gong ban yue kan*禹貢半月刊 (*The Evolution of Chinese Historical Geography*) 5卷 3–4期 (1936).

A pioneering article that shows strong interest in Chinese scholarship on Ricci's world map.

D'Elia, Pasquale M. *Il Mappamondo Cinese del P. Matteo Ricci*. Città del Vaticano: Biblioteca Apostolica Vaticana, 1938.

D'Elia, Pasquale M. "Recent Discoveries and New Studies, 1938–1960, on the World Map in Chinese of Father Matteo Ricci." *Monumenta Serica* (1961).

The editor of Ricci's papers here analyzes the copy of Ricci's world map in the collection of the Vatican Library.

Huang, Shijian 黄时鉴, and Gong, Yingyan 龚缨宴. *Li Madou shi jie di tu yan jiu* 利玛窦世界地图研究 (*Studies on the World Map of Ricci*). Shanghai: Shang hai gu ji chu ban she, 2004.

A recent and comprehensive study of the impact of Ricci's map with a detailed bibliography in the appendix.

Huang, Shijian 黄时鉴. "Li Madou shi jie di tu tan yuan lin zhua" 利玛窦世界地图探源鳞爪 ("Some Notes on the Origins of Ricci's World Map"). *Jiu zhou xue lin*九州学林 (*Chinese Culture Quarterly*) 3卷1期 (2005): 154–81.

A study of the editions, reception, and significance of the best-known map printed in China.

Hung, William 洪煨蓮. "Li Madou de shi jie di tu"「利瑪竇的世界地圖」("The World Map of Ricci"). *Yu gong ban yue kan* 禹貢半月刊 (*The Evolution of Chinese Historical Geography*) 5卷3–4期 (1936).

An introduction to Ricci's world map and its significance by a leading Chinese geographer.

Li, Zhaoliang 李兆良. *Kun yu wan guo quan tu jie mi: Ming dai ce hui shi jie* 坤輿萬國全圖解密：明代測繪世界 (台北 (*Unlocking the Secrets of Ricci's World Map: The Ming Dynasty Explores the World*). Taipei: Lianjing 聯經, 2012.

An updated and good synthesis of research on Ricci's world map for a general readership.

Ricci, Matteo. "Kun yu wan guo quan tu" 坤輿萬國全圖 (Complete Map of the Ten Thousand Countries of the World). Library of Congress. Geography and Map Division. National Digital Library Program. Beijing, 1602; Library of Congress, 2010. http://www.loc.gov/item/2010585650.

Yang, Yulei 杨雨蕾. "Li Madou shi jie di tu chuan ru han guo ji qi ying xiang" 「利玛窦世界地图传入韩国及其影响」 ("The Importation of Ricci's World Map to Korea and Its Impact"). *Zhong guo li shi di li lun cong* 中国历史地理论丛 (*Studies on Chinese Historical Geography*) 20卷1辑 (2005): 91–98

A study of the transmission and impact of Ricci's map to Yi dynasty Korea.

Modern Studies

In addition to biographies of Ricci, this section also lists the most important studies on Ricci's circle: his fellow Jesuit missionaries Valignano, Ruggieri, and Pantoja, and his most important Chinese collaborator, Xu Guangqi.

Bernard, Henri. *Le Père Matthieu Ricci et la société chinoise de son temps 1552–1610*. 2 vols. Tianjin: Hautes Études, 1937.

Written on the basis of Pietro Tacchi-Venturi's 1913 edition of Ricci's work, this study offers a biographical account of Ricci while introducing Ming China to readers in the West.

Chen, Weiping 陈卫平, and Li, Chunyong 李春勇. *Xu Guangqi ping zhuan* 徐光启评传 (A Critical Biography of Xu Guangqi). Nanjing: Nan jing da xue chu ban she, 2006.

Presents the career of Xu Guangqi in all its facets, with an emphasis on his official and scientific achievements.

Criveller, Gianni, and Guillén-Nuñez, César. *Portrait of a Jesuit: Matteo Ricci*. Macao: Ricci Institute, 2010.

A short book that contains four essays on Ricci's life, achievements, and the art and architecture associated with him.

Cronin, Vincent. *The Wise Man from the West: The True Story of the Man Who First Brought Christianity to Fabled Cathay.* New York: Image Books, 1955.

A lively book that is essentially an amplification of Ricci's *Della entrata.*

Fang, Hao方豪. *Zhong guo tian zhu jiao ren wu zhuan* 中國天主教史人物傳 (Biographies of Chinese Catholicism). 3 vols. Hong Kong: Zhong hua shu ju, 1970.

The first volume of this work contains biographies of leading western missionaries and Chinese converts at the time of Ricci.

Fontana, Michela. *Matteo Ricci: Un gesuita alla corte dei Ming.* Milan: Mondadori, 2005.

A lively book that emphasizes Ricci's cultural and scientific achievements.

Hsia, R. Po-chia 夏伯嘉. "Li Madou yu Zhang Huang" 利玛窦与章潢」 ("Ricci and Zhang Huang"). In *Wei le wen hua yu li shi: Yu Yingshi jiao shou ba zhi shou qing lun wen ji* 为了文化与历史: 余英时教授八秩寿庆论文集 (For Culture and History: Festschrift for Professor Yu Yingshi on His 80th Birthday). Taipei: Liang jing chu ban she, 2009, pp. 727–49.

An analysis of the impact of Zhang Huang on Ricci's synthesis of Confucianism and Christianity.

Hsia, R. Po-chia. "Valignano e Cina." In *Alessandro Valignano, S.I.: Uomo del Rinascimento: Ponte tra Oriente e Occidente,* edited by Adolfo Tamburello, M. Antoni Ücerler, and Marisa Di Russo. Rome: Institutum Historicum Societatis Iesu, 2008, pp. 102–3.

A brief discussion of the importance of Valignano to the Jesuit China mission and his relations with Ruggieri and Ricci.

Hsia, R. Po-chia 夏伯嘉.「《利瑪竇中國札記》 Scielou 人名考」 "Li Madou Zhong guo Xai ji Scielou ren ming kao" ("Who Was 'Scielou' in the Fonti Ricciane?"). 中央研究院歷史語言研究所集刊

(Bulletin of the Institute of History and Philology) 83, no. 1 (2012): 97–120.

Identifies a key figure in Ricci's rise in the social ladder of success by enabling him to leave Guangdong for the north.

Jami, Catherine, Peter Engelfriet, and Gregory Blue, editors. *Statecraft and Intellectual Renewal in Late Ming China: The Cross-Cultural Synthesis of Xu Guangqi (1562–1633)*. Leiden: Brill, 2001.

These essays on Xu Guangqi focus on his mathematical and religious collaboration with Ricci.

Lattis, James M. *Between Copernicus and Galileo: Christopher Clavius and the Collapse of Ptolemaic Cosmology*. Chicago: University of Chicago Press, 1994.

Reliable scholarship on European astronomy at the time of Clavius, Ricci's professor of mathematics in Rome.

Laven, Mary. *Mission to China: Matteo Ricci and the Jesuit Encounter with the East*. London: Faber & Faber, 2011.

Good treatment of Ruggieri's place in history; otherwise relies on Ricci's western language writings.

Lin, Jinshui 林金水. *Li Madou yu zhong guo* 利玛窦与中国 (Ricci and China). Beijing: Zhong guo she hui ke xue chu ban she, 1996.

Pioneering study that uses literati writings to reconstruct the network of converts and admirers around Ricci.

Malatesta, Edward, and Zhiyu, Guo, editors. *Departed, Yet Present: Zhalan, the Oldest Christian Cemetery in Beijing*. Macao/San Francisco: Instituto Cultural de Macao/Ricci Institute, 1995.

Photos and inscriptions of the old Catholic cemetery in Beijing, where Ricci's tombstone stands.

Mignini, Filippo. *Matteo Ricci: Il chiosco delle Fenici*. Ancona: Il Lavoro Editoriale, 2004.

Written by a scholar in Macerata, this biography is particularly strong in evoking the ambience of Ricci's birthplace and his childhood.

Needham, Joseph. *Chinese Astronomy and the Jesuit Mission: An Encounter of Cultures.* London: The China Society, 1958.

The leading expert on Chinese science objectively discusses the contributions of Jesuit science to Chinese astronomy.

Shih, Joseph, S.J. *Le Pere Ruggieri et le probleme de l'evangelisation en Chine.* Rome: Pontifical Gregorian University, 1964.

This is only a partial publication of the author's dissertation. It is the only and best study of Ruggieri, a figure unjustly neglected in the history of Christianity in China.

Song, Liming 宋黎明. *Shen fu de xin zhuang: Li Madou zai zhong guo, 1582–1610* 神父的新装 : 利玛窦在中国, 1582–1610 (The New Dress of the Father: Ricci in China). Nanjing: Nan jing da xue chu ban she, 2011.

A solid biography that uses both Italian and Chinese sources, written by an exiled Chinese dissident.

Spence, Jonathan D. *The Memory Palace of Matteo Ricci.* New York: Viking Penguin, 1984.

A classic that tries to reconstruct the mental world of Ricci by calling upon the mnemonic techniques described in one of Ricci's Chinese books.

Turner, Rossella. "La figura e l'opera di Michele Ruggieri, S.J. Missionario Gesuita in Cina." Tesi di laurea in storia e civiltà dell'Estremo Oriente. Naples: Istituto Universitario Orientale di Napoli, 1984.

A BA thesis at the University of Naples (in typescript) at the library of the Archivum Romanum Societatis Iesu that follows Ruggieri's career after his return to Italy.

Zhang, Kai 张铠. *Pang Diwo yu zhong guo* 庞迪我与中国 (*Diego de Pantoja and China*). Beijing: Beijing tu shu guan chu ban she, 1997.

A solid piece of scholarship that reconstructs the life of Diego Pantoja based on Spanish and Chinese sources.

INDEX